The Liturgical Ministry of Deacons

Second Edition

Michael Kwatera, O.S.B.

LITURGICAL PRESS

Collegeville, Minnesota

www.litpress.org

Quotations from the documents of the Second Vatican Council, papal documents, and the General Instruction of the Liturgy of the Hours are taken from *Documents on the Liturgy 1963–1979: Conciliar, Papal, and Curial Texts* (Collegeville: Liturgical Press, 1982) © 1982, International Committee on English in the Liturgy, Inc. All rights reserved.

Excerpts from the English translation of *The Roman Missal* © 1973, International Committee on the Liturgy, Inc. (ICEL); excerpts from the English translation of the *Order of Christian Funerals* © 1989, 1985, ICEL; excerpts from the English translation of the *Rite of Christian Initiation of Adults* © 1974, ICEL; excerpts from the English translation of the *Rite of Reception of Baptized Christians into Full Communion with the Catholic Church* © 1974, ICEL; excerpts from the English translation of the *Rite of Baptism for Children* © 1969, ICEL; excerpts from the English translation of the *Rite of Confirmation (Second Typical Edition)*, © 1975; excerpts from the English translation of the *Rite of Penance* © 1974, ICEL; excerpts from the *Rites of Ordination of a Bishop, of Priests, and of Deacons (Second Typical Edition)* © 2002, ICEL; excerpts from the English translation of the *General Instruction of the Roman Missal (Third Typical Edition)* © 2002, ICEL. All rights reserved.

1	2	3	4	5	6	7	8

Library of Congress Cataloging-in-Publication Data

Kwatera, Michael.
    The liturgical ministry of deacons / Michael Kwatera. — 2nd ed.
      p. cm.
    Includes bibliographical references.
    ISBN 13: 978-0-8146-3050-1 (pbk. : alk. paper)
    ISBN 10: 0-8146-3050-2 (pbk. : alk. paper)
    1. Deacons—Catholic Church.   I. Title.

BX1912.K93   2005
264'.02—dc22   2004020363

*Dedicated to
the inquisitive Deacon Peter
and to his patient bishop
and former deacon of Rome,
Gregory the Great,
whose dialogue reveals holy Benedict the abbot
as the "man of God"*

Contents

Preface

On December 4, 1983, the bishops of the United States approved a pastoral statement commemorating the twentieth anniversary of Vatican II's Constitution on the Sacred Liturgy. In commenting on the need for liturgical formation of the whole Christian community, they emphasized that

> bishops, priests and deacons must be helped . . . to understand better what they are doing when they celebrate the liturgy, to live the liturgical life more profoundly, and to share it effectively with others. They have a special responsibility to be formed in the spirit of the liturgy. . . . Deacons and other liturgical ministers . . . require a formation that is at once personally profound and directed toward their service within the assembly.[1]

In commemorating the fortieth anniversary of the Constitution on the Sacred Liturgy, Pope John Paul II observed that "it is more necessary than ever to promote the liturgical life within our communities, through an adequate formation of the ministers and of all the faithful, in view of that full, conscious and active participation in the liturgical celebrations envisioned by the Council."[2]

This book is offered to all deacons (both permanent and transitional) in the hope that it will promote their formation

---

1. *The Church at Prayer: A Holy Temple of the Lord* (Washington: United States Catholic Conference, 1984) nos. 11 and 12; 5.

2. *Apostolic Letter of the Supreme Pontiff John Paul II on the Fortieth Anniversary of the Constitution "Sacrosanctum Concilium" on the Sacred Liturgy*, no. 7.

for service within the Church's Eucharist, other sacramental rites, and communal prayer. It explains what deacons do within the liturgy and how they can do it effectively.

I express sincere thanks to Rev. Allan Bouley, O.S.B., from whom I learned much of what this book contains, and to the generous ordained and non-ordained ministers of the Church who read the manuscript and made helpful suggestions for its improvement.

Michael Kwatera, O.S.B.

Feast of St. Lawrence, Deacon and Martyr
August 10, 2004

Introduction

The Deacon's Liturgical Ministry: Past and Present

St. Ignatius, bishop of Antioch, apparently thought the world of his assistants, the deacons, and he didn't mind telling people. As he journeyed to martyrdom in Rome around the year 107, he wrote seven letters that reflect his high regard for deacons. Writing to the Magnesians, Ignatius calls them "my special favorites" (6:1); in his letter to the Philadelphians, he names them "my fellow slaves" (4:1). He explains to the Trallians that the deacons' service to the local church clearly shows them to "represent Jesus Christ, just as the bishop has the role of the Father, and the presbyters are like God's council and an apostolic band" (3:1). To those who have such a privileged role of visibly representing the One who came to serve the needs of all, Ignatius gives some fatherly advice: "Deacons of Jesus Christ's 'mysteries' must give complete satisfaction to everyone. For they do not serve mere food and drink, but minister to God's Church. They must therefore avoid leaving themselves open to criticism, as they would shun fire" (Trallians, 2:3).[3]

The bishops at the Second Vatican Council shared Ignatius's esteem for the ministry of deacons, as they declared in their Dogmatic Constitution on the Church: "Strengthened by sacramental grace they have as their service for the people of God,

3. Ignatius, "The Letters of Ignatius, Bishop of Antioch," in *Early Christian Fathers*, ed. and trans. Cyril C. Richardson (New York: The Macmillan Company, 1970) 95, 108–9, 99.

1

in communion with the bishop and his college of presbyters, the *diakonia* of liturgy, word, and charity" (no. 29). Yet the bishops noted that "as the discipline of the Latin Church currently stands, these diaconal functions, supremely necessary to the Church's life, can be carried out in many places only with great difficulty. Henceforth, therefore, it will be permissible to restore the diaconate as a distinct and permanent rank of the hierarchy" (*Ibid.*).

In *Sacrum diaconatus ordinem* (*motu proprio* of June 18, 1967), Pope Paul VI responded to widespread desire to restore the permanent diaconate in the Latin Church by allowing national episcopal conferences to do so. The service to God's Church that marked the lives of early deacons could now be continued in their successors' ministry of the liturgy, of the Gospel, and of works of charity, which the early history of diaconal ministry reveals to be interrelated and complementary.

The twelve apostles, with the unanimous consent of the Christian community, appointed seven "deeply spiritual and prudent" men to the task of distributing food, and strengthened them for this ministry by prayer and the laying on of hands (Acts 6:1-6). It is not clear whether Stephen and his companions were ordained deacons in the sense we would understand it today, but their functions have become the heart of diaconal ministry at the tables of the needy and the table of the Lord. References to deacons and deaconesses in the Pauline letters (Rom 16:1; Phil 1:1; 1 Tim 3:8-13) testify to a more established diaconal ministry within the local church.

In the patristic era deacons often exercised real administrative authority as the secretaries and possible successors of bishops, as well as the preeminent agents of the community's care for suffering and deprived persons. "That some, if not all, members of the diaconal college were everywhere stewards of the church funds and of the alms collected for widows and orphans is beyond dispute."[4] In Rome seven deacons were responsible for the

---

4. *The Catholic Encyclopedia*, 1908 ed., s.v. "Deacon" by Herbert Thurston.

care of needy Christians in the city's seven geographical divisions; either the bishop or the chief deacon kept a list of those who received the Church's charity. After each celebration of the Eucharist, deacons distributed the people's unused offerings (bread, wine, and other gifts) to the clergy and to needy persons.

As ministers of the Gospel, deacons instructed the catechumens preparing for baptism and assisted at their baptismal rites. Around the year 215 Hippolytus gave the following direction for the Roman baptismal liturgy: "Let a deacon carry the Oil of Exorcism and stand on the left hand. And another deacon shall take the Oil of Thanksgiving and stand on the right hand."[5] Also, a deacon was to accompany each candidate for baptism into the pool of water. If there were insufficient priests, deacons helped minister Communion to the newly baptized. Yet throughout the early centuries of the Church, deacons (as well as priests) were not permitted to baptize apart from grave necessity, though they might have done so occasionally as the bishop's deputies. Later, when the baptism of infants generally superseded the baptism of adults, deacons continued to have a significant role of assisting at the ceremonies. In the so-called Gelasian Sacramentary (ca. 750 in Gaul), deacons read the opening passages of the four Gospels to the infants and introduced the Lord's Prayer to them;[6] although a deacon asked the infants to "stand in silence and listen attentively," probably they were anything but silent and attentive.

As the Church's worship developed after Christianity became a tolerated (and later official) religion, deacons acquired a more prominent liturgical role. Serving as guardians of good order in the assembly, "they saw that the faithful occupied their proper places, that none gossiped or slept. They were to welcome the poor and the aged and to take care that they were not at a disadvantage as regards their position in church."[7] In

---

5. Hippolytus, *The Apostolic Tradition*, XXI:8, in *Documents of the Baptismal Liturgy*, ed. and trans. E. C. Whitaker (London: S.P.C.K., 1977) 5.

6. The Gelasian Sacramentary XXXIV, XXXVI, in Whitaker, 172–74, 177–79.

7. "Deacon" by Thurston.

the crowded basilicas deacons lifted up their voices to give directions to worshipers, and indicated the external and internal attitudes they should assume: "Wisdom! Let us be attentive!"; "Let us kneel . . . . let us stand"; "Salute one another with the holy kiss"; "Go, the Mass is ended." Yet these helpful directions sometimes went unheeded. Bishop Caesarius of Arles (470–547) admonished his congregation:

> I have carefully noted that when the deacon says the usual *flectamus genua* ["Let us kneel."] most of the people frequently remain standing like straight columns. This is not at all proper or right for Christians who are praying in church, because the deacon does not pray for us but for you. Since those words are addressed to you in particular and most of all to the negligent, it is just for you to devoutly obey them.[8]

Clearly, Caesarius wanted the deacon's intercessory prayer and the assembly's gesture of assent to form a single, united act of supplication.

Deacons read the Scripture lessons, especially the gospel, at the Eucharist, but apparently preached very rarely or not at all. It was also the deacon's function to lead the general intercessions by bidding the assembly to pray for intentions which he announced in a litany.

After the people had presented their offerings of bread and wine, deacons prepared the table and gifts. In both East and West these assistants at the altar held a special relation to the sacred vessels and gifts, both before and after the consecration. As early as around the year 150, St. Justin Martyr noted in his description of the Eucharist at Rome: "When the president has finished his eucharist and the people have all signified their assent, those whom we call 'deacons' distribute the bread and the wine and water over which the eucharist has been spoken,

---

8. Caesarius, Sermon 77, "Another Admonition by This Same Ephrem to Bend the Knee in Prayer, and on Idle Gossip," trans. Mary Magdeleine Mueller, in the Father of the Church series, vol. 31 (New York: The Fathers of the Church, 1956) 355.

to each of those present; they also carry them to those who are absent" (due to illness or imprisonment for their faith).[9] Ministering the cup of the Lord's Blood seems to have been a special part of the office of deacons.

Besides assisting at the Eucharist, deacons exercised a similarly important role in the public services of morning and evening prayer that became a regular part of the Church's worship in the fourth century. Egeria, a Spanish nun who made a pilgrimage to the Holy Land around the year 385, described the evening service in Jerusalem to her sisters back home. After the assembly has finished singing the appointed psalms and antiphons, "one of the deacons makes the normal commemoration of individuals, and each time he mentions a name a large group of boys responds *Kyrie eleison* (in our language, Lord, have mercy). Their voices are very loud. As soon as the deacon has done his part, the bishop says a prayer and prays the Prayer for All."[10] The deacon probably announced the intentions and the assembly responded; then the deacon called the assembly to kneel for silent prayer before the bishop summed up the petitions in a concluding prayer. Once again, the deacon's constant concern for the suffering members of the community made him the logical minister to lead prayers for them.

The fruitful union of liturgical ministry within the assembly and charitable service outside it is clearly attested in the life and death of St. Lawrence, deacon and martyr.[11] During Valerian's persecution in 258, Sixtus II, bishop of Rome, was led

9. Justin, *Apologia I*, in Lucien Deiss, *Springtime of the Liturgy: Liturgical Tests of the First Four Centuries*, trans. Matthew J. O'Connell (Collegeville: Liturgical Press, 1979) 92.

10. *Egeria's Travels to the Holy Land*, 24:5-6, trans. John Wilkinson, rev. ed. (Jerusalem: Ariel Publishing House; Warminster, England: Aris & Phillips, 1981) 124.

11. The details in the following account are drawn from *Butler's Lives of the Saints*, vol. VIII, ed. Herbert Thurston and Donald Attwater (New York: P. J. Kenedy & Sons, 1933) 123–26 and *The Golden Legend of Jacobus de Voragine*, trans. and adapted by Granger Ryan and Helmut Ripperger (New York: Longmans, Green and Co., Inc., 1941) 437–45.

away to imprisonment and death. Lawrence, Rome's chief deacon, followed after him, weeping and crying out: "Father, where are you going without your son? Should the priest go to sacrifice without the deacon? Never have you offered sacrifice without a minister!" While this speech may be apocryphal, it certainly illustrates the coordinated action of different yet complementary ministries within the early Roman liturgy, and something more: Lawrence realized that Bishop Sixtus was about to complete the worship he had offered to God in the Eucharist by offering his own life in martyrdom. Similarly, the holy deacon also wanted to reproduce Christ's self-sacrifice in himself—the sacrifice that he regularly ministered to God's people in the cup of the Lord's Blood. He was to receive his wish, just as Sixtus foretold: "I do not leave you, my son. You shall follow me in three days."

Having seized the Church's leader, the Roman prefect moved quickly to seize the Church's treasures. He sent his soldiers to apprehend Lawrence, whose care for the poor apparently had been evident to all, even to the Church's enemies, and commanded him to hand over the treasures; Lawrence told him that he would need three days' time to do so. Rome's chief deacon lost no time in seeking out the poor, widows, and orphans, and shared among them the money he was administering. On the third day Lawrence made good on his promise: he gathered a great number of the city's poor and placed them in rows: the elderly, the blind, the lame, lepers, orphans, widows. Then, instead of handing over silver and gold, Lawrence presented these lowly ones to the eyes of the greedy official: "Here are the true treasures of the Church." This bold affirmation of their surpassing Christian dignity, which came easily from a man who had faithfully ministered the Lord's Blood and the Lord's charity to them, won him a painful but glorious death on the gridiron. St. Augustine linked Lawrence's self-sacrifice in martyrdom with his self-giving in the Eucharist:

> Lawrence, as you have heard, fulfilled the office of deacon in the church of Rome. There he ministered the sacred Blood of Christ,

there he poured out his blood for the sake of Christ. . . . The holy apostle John has clearly revealed the mystery of the Lord's Supper by telling us: "As Christ laid down his life for us, so we must lay down our lives for our brothers." St. Lawrence grasped that teaching; he understood it and practiced it. In a word, what he received at that table, he prepared to fulfill in himself. He loved Christ during life and imitated him in death.[12]

The story of St. Lawrence shows that the liturgical ministry of deacons ideally was a seal they placed on their other duties.[13]

The medieval Church suffered a decline in appreciation of the vital bond between service of God in the liturgy and service of others outside it; the social ministry of deacons diminished and their liturgical ministry increased. "As deacons became much more liturgical in function, they became more priestly in lifestyle. By the tenth century, the diaconate as a separate order and office in the church had all but disappeared."[14] Alexander Kniazeff explains that as a result the diaconate "became simply a theoretical step on the hierarchic ladder, with individuals being obliged to stay on it for only a brief moment of the journey toward priestly ordination."[15] The post-Vatican II renewal of the permanent diaconate is an attempt to restore the ancient and revered vocation of deacon to its proper place in the liturgy, administration, and social ministry of the local church.

Clearly, both transitional and permanent deacons engage in a cluster of activities—some within the liturgy, some outside it—that complement and intensify each other. The important

12. Augustine, *Sermo CCCIV in solemnitate Laurentii martyris*, III, in *Patrologiae Latinae*, XXXVIII, ed. J.-P. Migne (Paris, 1863) co. 1595.

13. For a more detailed presentation of the deacon's liturgical ministry in the early Church, see J. Robert Wright, "The Emergence of the Diaconate," *Liturgy*, vol. 2, no. 4: Diakonia (Fall 1982) 17–23, 67–71.

14. Americus Roy, "The Ministry of Service," in *Liturgy*, vol. 2, no. 4: Diakonia (Fall 1982) 61.

15. Alexander Kniazeff, "The Role of the Deacon in the Byzantine Liturgical Assembly," *Roles in the Liturgical Assembly*, trans. Matthew J. O'Connell (New York: Pueblo Publishing Company, 1981) 167–68.

ecumenical document of the World Council of Churches, *Baptism, Eucharist and Ministry* (1982), highlights such interrelatedness while summarizing what various Christian traditions believe the ministry of deacons to be: "Deacons represent to the Church its calling as servant in the world. By struggling in Christ's name with the myriad needs of societies and persons, deacons exemplify the interdependence of worship and service in the Church's life."[16]

While this booklet focuses on the deacon's liturgical ministry to God's people at the Eucharist and other services, such ministry is ideally the seal that he reverently and lovingly places on his other ministries of caring for their bodily and spiritual needs. Diaconal service within the liturgy is the climax and celebration of diaconal service outside it: "The deacon serves in liturgy because the deacon serves in the Church. Service to those in need . . . focuses outwardly and visibly through the liturgical words and actions of the deacon. In this way, among several ways, the world enters into the liturgy and is presented to God, and in this way, too, the deacon reveals the servanthood of Christ in which the people are to share."[17]

The liturgy is the source from which the effectiveness of diaconal ministry flows and the summit to which it is directed (cf. the Constitution on the Sacred Liturgy, no. 10). There should be no conflict between these two necessary and complementary forms of ministry; rather, there should be the greatest harmony between them, as Joe Morris Doss explains:

> In proclaiming the gospel, the deacon represents our awareness that the good news is not only for edification in worship and for awareness of eschatological salvation, but for our daily living, a present in which Christ gives us more abundant life. Leading our prayers, the deacon is the dominant sign of the

16. *Baptism, Eucharist and Ministry*, Faith and Order Paper No. 111, no. 31 (Geneva: World Council of Churches, 1982) 27.

17. Ormande Plater, *The Deacon in the Liturgy* (Boston: National Center for the Diaconate, 1981) 2–3.

ministry of the church as servant to the world. Inviting confession, the deacon magnifies our calling to be those who live for others in God's love and our need to confess our failures to love. Receiving our offerings, the deacon assists us to be more visually aware that the bread, the wine, and the monetary offerings represent our total lives, our daily living—not just what we give and do for the institutional church.

Preparing the table, the deacon embodies our ministry in the concrete sense of the original usage of the word *diakonos*. We are humble people of God serving as though waiters. The distribution of the sacrament, like the proclamation of the gospel, grants us not only to taste the kingdom in our sanctification, but to be nourished in and for our daily lives of service. Finally, when the officer of service gives the dismissal, it is a sign that the people of God are together in worship and ready to go out into the world in the love and service of Christ.[18]

The deacon's liturgical ministry, which must be wedded to his social ministry, is outlined in Pope Paul VI's *Sacrum diaconatus ordinem*, which restored the permanent diaconate in the Latin Church (no. 22):

1. to assist the bishop and priest during liturgical services in regard to all those matters assigned to the deacon by the liturgical books for the various rites;
2. to administer baptism solemnly . . . .;
3. to reserve the eucharist and to give communion to himself and others; to bring viaticum to the dying; to give benediction with the monstrance or ciborium;
4. to assist at marriages in the name of the Church, when no priest is available, and, with the bishop's or pastor's delegation, to impart the nuptial blessing. . . .;
5. to administer sacramentals and preside at funerals and burial rites;
6. to read the books of Scripture to the faithful, to instruct and exhort the congregation;

18. Joe Morris Doss, "The Ordination of Deacons," in *Liturgy*, vol. 2, no. 4: Diakonia (Fall 1982) 15–16.

7. to preside at offices of worship and at prayer services, when no priest is available;

8. to lead celebrations of the Word, especially in places where there is a lack of priests.

Such is the liturgical service that deacons render to God and God's people in the celebration of the Eucharist, other sacramental rites, and communal prayer, for which this booklet offers some directions and suggestions. In using it may they set a seal on their many diverse expressions of self-giving as did Jesus Christ, whose ministering the new covenant in his Blood sealed his entire life of self-sacrifice and remains the necessary pattern for those who minister in his name.

Flying Duo in the Liturgy

Perhaps you have had this experience: sitting in an airplane, awaiting take-off, and observing, through the opened door or curtain between the flight deck and the rest of the aircraft, the pilot and copilot (usually called the captain and first officer) sitting side-by-side, preparing for departure: throwing switches; pushing buttons; checking the instrument panel; and reviewing charts, flight plan, and weather reports. Once the flight is underway, it is usually the captain who addresses the passengers and reports only the tiniest fraction of all that information. But it has always been reassuring for me to know that the captain has the able assistance of another expert in all the details of flying in general and of this flight in particular. The captain ultimately is always in charge (and thus blamed for everything) but somehow I like to think that both the captain and first officer are better for having the presence and assistance of the other.

In a sense, every liturgy is a kind of flight: not a flight of measurable miles, but an immeasurable flight of the spirit. The liturgy is a flight both divine and human that takes us to the very throne room of God. There we join angels and saints in worship that is a pattern for our earthly one. This flight is one that worshipers of all times and places have made before us. And surely deacons must know much about the details of this flight. Their role of giving directions, proclaiming the gospel, and ministering at the altar has led some commentators to compare them to angels, those winged messengers from God to God's people. Angels know how to fly, so deacons must too.

Every liturgy is a flight: from the take-off (the gathering, the opening hymn, and the introductory rites) to the landing (the blessing and dismissal that send us forth), worshipers make a spiritual journey through the Scripture readings and homily, pray for the well-being of fellow travelers in the intercessions, share welcome and necessary nourishment in the Eucharist, and then reach a destination that always begins another journey: going out to share the liturgy's gifts with the world that needs them. And for this frequent, at least weekly, flight the ideal is a pilot and copilot, a captain and first officer, a priest and a deacon, two fellow servants of God and God's assembly. Their ministry together produces something greater than the ministry of each. As in every flight, so in every liturgy, the priest ultimately is responsible for all aspects of the celebration. That is why he is called the *presider*. But on our liturgical flights, unlike on other flights, the copilot or first officer, the deacon, addresses the passengers at very significant moments, for very significant purposes, and even helps serve the meal of holy food and drink. And his proclamation of the gospel and his preaching make him a real angel, a real messenger, of God's good news to humankind. In every word and act of his liturgical ministry, he takes up where the angel at Bethlehem and the angel at the tomb of the risen Christ left off: "Don't be afraid! Jesus Christ is Lord!" The Eastern churches fittingly put the words, "Wisdom! Be attentive!" into the deacon's mouth before he proclaims the gospel. What a privilege is his: to offer wisdom, God's hidden wisdom, God's saving wisdom to a world that often seems bereft of true wisdom or hostile to it. Truly it is a task for angels and for those who represent their ministry within the liturgy.

Sometimes our liturgies seem much more earthly than heavenly. Sometimes our liturgical flights are smooth and satisfying; sometimes boring; sometimes bumpy. Clearly, in our liturgical flights as in our air travel, the captain and first officer have much to do with how smooth and satisfying the trip will be. The document *Music in Catholic Worship* reminds us that "Good celebrations foster and nourish faith. Poor celebrations may weaken and destroy it" (no. 6). These words should be lettered out and placed in a prominent place in every sacristy, so that liturgical ministers might see them before every liturgy. The ministry of the liturgy's captain and first officer bears a significant privilege and a significant responsibility in this regard. And just as the word "liturgy" needs a "u" in the middle, so the liturgy looks for you and me, needs you and me.

The liturgy looks for the ministry of the deacon because his liturgical ministry puts a kind of seal on all the other service that he gives to the people of God. His liturgical ministry is a bit like that classic definition of a sacrament: an outward sign of inner grace. The deacon's liturgical service brings to the eyes and ears of all an image of his service to others that may be less visible and audible to some in the community. Rev. Timothy Shugrue rightly explains that

> The deacon's faithfulness to his charitable ministry will help to validate his ministries of liturgy and the Word. When he appears as a liturgical minister, as presider or in an assisting role, it should be plain that he brings to the experience of worship those for whom he has been caring, and that he stands as a witness to their claim on our compassion. When he proclaims or expounds the Word, in whatever setting, his ministry must resonate with echoes of the voices of need he has listened to and must yield evidence of his firsthand struggle to speak the good news to those who may have begun to lose hope. Thus are the several expressions of the deacon's ministry integrated in a unified witness to the abiding presence of the Servant Christ.[19]

The ministry of a deacon within the liturgy can make that liturgy more ritually full as well as more smooth. Many, perhaps most, eucharistic liturgies are celebrated without the

---

19. Rev. Timothy J. Shugrue, *Service Ministry of the Deacon* (Washington, D.C.: United States Catholic Conference, 1988) 42–43.

ministry of a deacon, with no harm to the efficacy of the sacramental celebration. But the "people's" in the "people's work," the liturgy, is underscored when the liturgy's captain and first officer together exercise a leadership role of service.

What the Church teaches about receiving Communion under forms of both bread and wine parallels the complementary ministries of the priest and deacon within the liturgy. It is true, as the Council of Trent taught in the sixteenth century, that "Christ, whole and entire, exists under the species of bread and under any part of that species, and similarly the whole Christ exists under the species of wine and under its parts."[20] Thus, to receive the whole Christ in Holy Communion, one need receive only one species or part thereof. Yet the General Instruction of the Roman Missal (2002) states that "Holy Communion has a fuller form as a sign when it is distributed under both kinds. For in this form the sign of the Eucharistic banquet is more clearly evident" (no. 281). In applying this to the deacon's role in the liturgy, I would emend this last sentence to read: "For in this form of celebration—a priest and deacon ministering together—the *service*-sign of the Eucharistic banquet is more clearly evident."

What does the deacon bring to this service-sign? Not just his service in speaking words, giving invitations to the assembly, and handling objects within the liturgy, but also the service he gives to others outside the liturgy. Timothy Shugrue is correct: "Perhaps one way of describing this 'distinctive and necessary' service is to suggest that diaconate is essential because it embodies or expresses, in the particularly concentrated form of a ritual sign, the image or character of the Church as servant."[21]

Every follower of Jesus is called to serve God and neighbor. Yet some are called to be special servants at the Eucharist: they are among their fellow worshipers as those who serve the rest.

20. Council of Trent, *Decree on the Most Holy Eucharist*, ch. IV. *Transubstantiation*. DS 1640/TCT 721.

21. Shugrue, 21.

At the Eucharist, just as at Thanksgiving dinner, some members of the family accept the responsibility of preparing the meal and serving it to the other members of the family. *All* are family, but some are servants and some are guests for that occasion. Similarly, the Eucharist unites the worshipers in the festive meal of God's family, but some worshipers help express that unity through their service to others.

Thus, servants at the Eucharist, and especially those who serve as deacons, cannot lose sight of their oneness with the priest as he serves the assembly in their worship, yet they can never lose sight of their oneness with their fellow worshipers. As deacons minister within the liturgy, they are a clear sign that the liturgy does not belong to the presiding priest alone. Rather, liturgical leadership, like the liturgy itself, is the people's work, not one person's work, not even one ordained priest's work. Here again, the deacon's liturgical ministry is an outward sign of inner grace, an outward expression of the liturgy's innermost heart.

Delight in belonging to God's family assembled for worship enables the deacon to fulfill the tasks of preparing persons (for example, servers) and spaces for the celebration, extending hospitality, proclaiming the gospel, preaching, giving directions, and sharing Communion, as well as any special or unusual demands that develop during the liturgical flight: like getting up to light the candles or turn on the lights or microphone when no one else does, or getting a book or vessel that is needed, or adjusting the temperature in the worship space (and I'm not thinking here of fire-and-brimstone sermons!). In all such tasks, in everything the deacon does or speaks within the liturgy, it is his to say by his example: "It certainly has been our privilege to have you on board today." Isn't that what liturgical service is for?

But there is a sense in which the deacon's service within every liturgical flight begins outside the liturgy, begins well in advance of the liturgy. There is a sense in which every sacramental celebration is the culmination of a process that begins long before the actual liturgy: the process of preparing the liturgy itself, but more importantly, preparing people to participate fully, consciously, and actively in sacramental celebrations. Here is where the deacon's ministry to the Christian community, especially its poorest and weakest members, is so important and so necessary.

Timothy Shugrue rightly explains that

> . . . a continuing liturgical or homiletic practice in one particular parish community should have as a prerequisite a dimension of charitable service, well-recognized by that community. This is so that the deacon's ministries of liturgy and the Word can achieve their full potential for nourishing the community, as ritual expressions of that call to service of neighbor which is a constitutive element of the Christian life.[22]

Service: a constitutive element of Christian life, not a luxury or an option, and thus a constitutive element of Christian liturgy as well. As the deacon serves the assembly as their first officer, he completes his service to them outside the liturgy. He has much to do with whether and how the assembly will be able to say and mean these words: "It is right to give God thanks and praise." Here is wonderful testimony to the deacon's relationship to the captain of the liturgy, the priest: diaconal ministry will have much to do with how powerfully the priest can proclaim the great Eucharistic Prayer in the name of all, praising God for the divine goodness and victory even in the face of family difficulties, personal and global tragedies, poverty, illness, and death. But we never minister alone. Jesus Christ ministers with us and in us, as Edward McKenna reminds us in a hymn text: "With the sick, needy, old, humbled poor, / May our works of love and care endure. / What we weakly perform in Christ's name, / He remakes in peace as strong and pure."[23]

---

22. Ibid., 53.
23. Edward J. McKenna, "The Paschal Hymn," v. 3, in *The Collegeville Hymnal* (Collegeville: Liturgical Press, 1990) no. 281.

Within the liturgical celebration itself, servants must expect to participate a bit differently from guests, because servants have accepted a special responsibility to represent the Lord Jesus, whose self-giving must be the pattern for their own. But this does not give the ministers exclusive ownership of the feast; captain and first officer are to be responsible for the liturgy along with the other ministers but not possessive of it. They are to be like the Communion cups that freely offer the precious gift of self-sacrificing love to others. "It is a privilege to have you on board today" is what ministers should love to say to people they love, and should say more lovingly each time they minister.

The reaffirmation of faith that every liturgy is meant to be flows out of our own faith in Christ, the faith that we manifest in our service to others outside and inside the liturgy. Here is a great privilege and a great responsibility that, for a deacon, begins within his own family. Deacons minister within two churches: their domestic church and their local church. In Charles Balsam's words: the deacon "has the potential of helping both churches understand each other in view of the paschal mystery, and to foster a partnership in disciple making. I can think of no greater pastoral challenge."[24] Deacons share with their wives a unique opportunity to bridge church and home in liturgical celebration. They can help insure that parish worship in church enhances family worship at home, and vice versa.

---

24. Charles Balsam, "The Family—Our First Community," in *Deacon Digest*, vol. 12, no. 1 (January–February 1995) 25.

Some Preliminaries

Vesting

The ancient link between deacons and bishops is preserved in the dalmatic, a long tunic with wide sleeves that has become the Roman deacon's proper vestment. "The more common opinion holds that at first only the pope wore it; he gradually allowed others (the Roman deacons first of all in the fourth century) to wear it as a privilege."[25]

In the East and in Gaul, a stole worn over the left shoulder was the symbol of diaconal ministry. In antiquity the stole was a long scarf worn by such official persons as messengers. Recipients of letters could tell from a distance the identity of the senders because of the messengers' distinctive stoles. In the same way the deacon's stole marked him as one sent by Jesus Christ as herald of his Gospel. When the Gallican Church adopted the dalmatic, both dalmatic and stole became the deacon's customary vestments. The Roman Church has long accepted this blend of Eastern and Roman usages for its own use.

The alb and amice (an oblong piece of white cloth worn around the neck and under the alb) have long been the liturgical underclothing of clerics. Rather sheer albs should be worn only under a dalmatic. If a deacon is to wear only a stole over the alb, the latter should be of such fabric that street clothes do not show through, and it should be of such length that it reaches the tops of his shoes (preferably black shoes). The alb

25. *New Catholic Encyclopedia*, 1967 ed., s.v. "Dalmatic" by M. McCance.

may have a collar or cowl that fills in unsightly gaps around the neck as it covers the shirt collar; but "before the alb is put on, should this not completely cover the ordinary clothing of the neck, an amice should be put on" (General Instruction of the Roman Missal [2002] = GI, no. 336).

The stole, in the color proper to the feast, season, or occasion, is worn over the left shoulder, drawn across the chest, and fastened at the right side (GI, no. 340). Liturgical authenticity requires that only a deacon of an Eastern rite should wear an Eastern-style *orarion* (a long, narrow stole that hangs down, back and front, from the left shoulder).

While the dalmatic, also of proper color, may be added in any liturgy, the most common vesture is simply an alb and stole. The dalmatic customarily has been reserved for occasions where greater solemnity is fitting, for example, in episcopal liturgies and Holy Week services. It is worn "over the alb and stole" (GI, no. 338), that is, the stole is worn *under* the dalmatic. Some vestment manufacturers are now offering white "all-purpose" dalmatics with over-stoles in the liturgical colors. Such an innovation seems to do injustice to the dalmatic: a wide, flowing garment whose distinctive shape announces the office of the one who wears it and whose color accents the feast, season, or occasion in a significant way.

Historically the deacon's dalmatic was a counterpart to the priest's chasuble at the Eucharist. Just as the priest generally does not wear the chasuble except when he presides at Mass, so the deacon should not wear the dalmatic when he presides at such services as baptisms, marriages, funerals, exposition and benediction of the Blessed Sacrament, or the Liturgy of the Hours. In such celebrations the deacon might wear a cope over the alb and stole. The deacon should practice functioning in the sanctuary while wearing this ample garment, so that he can determine how it may restrict his movements and require their adjustment. When presiding at baptisms, the deacon should push back the cope from his arms before pouring the water or immersing the candidate.

If present for the ordination of deacons or the funeral of a deacon, priest, or bishop, it may be fitting for deacons to wear an alb and stole even though they are not exercising their ministry. The Bishops' Committee on the Liturgy has explained in its *Study Text VI* that "since they are present for the celebration as members of the order of deacons, the wearing of their proper vestment may symbolize their collegiality with the other deacons. However, special consideration may be given in those situations when the families of married deacons are present,"[26] that is, married deacons may prefer to forego vesting so as to sit with their families, rather than vest and sit in a place apart. In any case possible confusion with priest-concelebrants is to be carefully avoided.

While most ordained ministers have favorite stoles (often lovingly made by relatives or friends as ordination gifts), care must be taken to ensure that such deacon stoles do not clash with the priest's vestments. Not all purples, reds, etc., are complementary, nor are all patterns and textures compatible. The informed judgment of artists and designers can help ensure that the vestments of priest, deacon, and other ministers, as well as banners in the worship space, are complementary in color and design. In some cases an extra priest's stole that matches the principal celebrant's vestments can be pinned for use as a deacon's stole. But those who are responsible for buying or making liturgical vestments for the parish should be encouraged to provide matching vestments for priest and deacon (including the dalmatic if possible). Perhaps it is best to save homemade stoles for services in which the deacon exercises his ministry alone, for example, presiding at baptisms and leading public prayer.

Even well-made vestments will not look good if they are worn poorly. Robert Hovda correctly states that "vesting requires the assistance of a full-length mirror or of another

---

26. Bishops' Committee on the Liturgy, *Study Text VI: The Deacon, Minister of Word and Sacrament* (Washington: United States Catholic Conference, 1979) 43.

person."[27] Priests and deacons should serve each other in this matter.

Light-reflecting pieces of jewelry, such as watches and rings, call unnecessary attention to themselves during ritual actions, and should be left in the sacristy or in a pocket. It is appropriate to wear a wedding band, however, because it symbolizes the unique blending of the sacraments of marriage and orders in the married permanent deacon. A transitional deacon should not wear any ring which may cause confusion regarding his celibate state.

Participating as a Member of the Assembly

In every liturgical celebration the first act of Christian worship is *gathering*. The assembly of worshipers is the basic liturgical symbol and primary liturgical minister: it incarnates the faith by which the members of the Body of Christ share in his self-offering to the Father. In the assembly the Church becomes visible, audible, and tangible as it does nowhere else, yet it does so with the assistance of those who exercise particular functions: priest, deacon, readers, extraordinary ministers of Holy Communion, choir, cantor, ushers, servers. The role of deacon requires that this minister be, first, an actively participating member of the assembly, one who delights in being an "insider":

> . . . all special ministers are, above all, members of the assembly. They must know this and show it. They have got to accept this identity. Failure to do so renders their ministry useless and sterile. Nobody can minister from the outside. You have to "belong" first. You have to know that you belong and you have to act in such a way that everybody else knows that you belong.[28]

27. Robert W. Hovda, "For Presiders/Preachers," *Touchstones for Liturgical Ministers*, ed. Virginia Sloyan (Washington: The Liturgical Conference, 1978) 27.

28. Eugene Walsh, *Giving Life: The Ministry of the Parish Sunday Assembly* (Old Hickory, Tenn.: Pastoral Arts Associates of North America, 1982) 11b–12a.

The deacon and the assembly are "made for each other," in the sense that his service to them should deepen their sense of being the Body of Christ, while their service to him should deepen his sense of being a fellow member of that Body. Every special liturgical ministry (including that of priest and deacon) exists for the sake of the primary minister, the assembly (not vice versa); the priest and deacon share the unique ministry of coordinating the other ministries for the full and active participation of all the members of Christ's Body.

Coordinating Ministries

"Assistance in liturgy is not a function performed only by deacons. It is shared by priests (other than the celebrant), readers, cantors, and acolytes."[29] In exercising his ministry at a number of different services with different priests, readers, and servers, the deacon will want to explain to them how his ministry relates to what they have been trained to do; such respect and courtesy for each minister will promote the teamwork of all ministers.

When functioning at the Sunday Eucharist, a decision must be made in advance about who will lead the general intercessions. Traditionally this is a diaconal role, but other circumstances (for example, the legitimate and welcome ministry of lay readers) may suggest that someone else should do this. It seems fitting that the deacon lead the intercessions on solemn occasions.

The deacon should explain to the servers that he is like an extra, "chief" server and alert them to the special aspects of his role (receiving the gifts, preparing the gifts and the altar) so that they won't be unduly confused; this can be an important exercise of the deacon's responsibility to keep good order in the service. He should be ready to signal the ushers if someone faints or needs medical attention.

29. Plater, 5.

If presiding (especially at the Liturgy of the Hours), it is good for the deacon to delegate to others some of his usual functions (for example, leading the intercessions and making announcements). Such sharing of functions shows that no one ministry exercises a monopoly.

Ministering with Other Deacons

The General Instruction of the Roman Missal states that "if there are several persons present who are able to exercise the same ministry, nothing forbids their distributing among themselves and performing different parts of the same ministry or duty. For example, one deacon may be assigned to take the sung parts, another to serve at the altar" (no. 109).

In October 1981, the Bishops' Committee on the Liturgy *Newsletter* recommended that "normally those deacons who are present, but not called upon to function in the celebration, should not vest or occupy a specific place in the liturgy. This will prevent the development of a practice that might easily appear to be an imitation of concelebration."[30] The following year, this *Newsletter* clarified this recommendation by noting that

> there *are* times when the deacons of a diocese *stand as an order*, in which case they *would* vest and be seated together in a specific place. The primary instance when this would be true is at the celebration of the ordination of another deacon. Other times when deacons might function as an order would be at the Mass of Christian Burial of a member of the diaconal order, and at various diocesan or regional celebrations. Even in these cases, however, as was the principal point being made in the earlier note, the deacons should remain in their assigned place during the liturgy of the eucharist in order to avoid any confusion of ministries between them and the priests who may be concelebrating the liturgy.[31]

30. Bishops' Committee on the Liturgy *Newsletter*, XVII (October 1981) 39.
31. Bishops' Committee on the Liturgy *Newsletter*, XVIII (July–August 1982) 31.

The trend seems to be away from such vesting, except at ordinations and a few other occasions. Local custom may dictate something other than what the guidelines recommend.

The Chrism Mass is a diocesan celebration wherein deacons might stand as an order. Many liturgists find this liturgy's renewal of priestly commitment by the bishop and priests to be problematic; thus, it is unclear whether a similar provision for deacons to renew their commitment to service as ordained ministers would be desirable. Some comparable formula, drawn up by the diocesan liturgical commission and approved by the bishop, might be included as part of this rite at the Chrism Mass, but only after careful study of this question by the diocesan liturgical commission in consultation with the deacons.

Making Friends with Rubrics

The liturgical books contain rubrics (directions for the priest and other ministers) that indicate what the deacon does and says during each service. They are friendly guides to lead the deacon and the assembly in the series of coordinated words and actions that comprises the Roman liturgy. The General Instruction of the Roman Missal (GI) at the front of the Roman Missal and the Order of Mass in the middle give the rubrics for the celebration of the Eucharist; the Roman Missal and Ceremonial of Bishops also provide helpful directions and notes for processions on certain days and for Holy Week liturgies. Rubrics and texts for the baptism of children, marriage, and funerals are found in separate ritual books. The Pontifical (the book containing texts for services at which the bishop presides) includes directions for deacons who minister at ordinations. These books provide liturgical "scripts" that the deacon will want to know well in order to exercise his ministry and to minimize or rectify awkward mistakes in liturgical services if they occur. Where there is no "master of ceremonies," the deacon should assume this task as well. If there is no other minister present, the deacon "fulfills the duties of other ministers himself" (GI, no. 171f.). Thus the deacon should always know what readings and prayer texts will be used, as well as the "cues," since he may become the "director" at any time.

Giving Directions

In accord with his responsibility for maintaining good order in the liturgy and for coordinating the functions of fellow ministers (including the primary one, the assembly), the deacon calls upon the worshipers to respond in prayer and extends an invitation to exchange the sign of peace. The deacon may also ask the assembly to begin the procession ("Let us go forth in peace"); to kneel for the penitential rite or solemn intercessions on Good Friday; to stand or sit if they are slow to do so; to bow their heads for the solemn blessing or the prayer over the people; and to go in peace.

In giving directions it seems best to put the request for a change of posture *last*. If the deacon says, "Let us kneel in prayer and ask for the Lord's mercy and forgiveness," people may begin to go down on their knees as soon as they hear "Let us kneel," thereby missing *why* they are being invited to kneel (to ask for the Lord's mercy and forgiveness). The second, important part of the invitation will be no match for the crashing of kneelers and the rustling of bodies. Thus, it is best to put first things first: "Let us humbly ask the Lord's mercy and forgiveness as we kneel in prayer." The deacon's subsequent gracious act of kneeling (along with the priest's) will speak its own invitation to the assembly to do the same. The deacon might choose to extend his hands in an inviting gesture directed toward the assembly while saying: "Let us . . . ." This modest gesture, different from the more expansive, *orans* ("praying") position assumed by the priest during the presidential prayers, can serve to give visible illustration to the words. The casualness of invitations like "Let's go in peace" is not compatible with the somewhat formal character of the Roman liturgy.

Exercising the ministry of giving directions requires sensitivity to the priest's manner of liturgical leadership and familiarity with the rhythm of each celebration. Observation of other good presiders and assistants, practice, and experience are good teachers in the art of giving warm yet undramatic invitations to the assembly. In this as in every matter of liturgical "style," smooth technique comes from practice; quality comes from sincerity and the proper understanding of the deacon's role.

The Deacon's Role in . . .

The Celebration of the Eucharist

Before Mass

After the priest, the deacon, in virtue of the sacred ordination he has received, holds first place among those who minister in the Eucharistic Celebration. For the sacred Order of the diaconate has been held in high honor in the Church even from the time of the Apostles. At Mass the deacon has his own part in proclaiming the Gospel, in preaching God's word from time to time, in announcing the intentions of the Prayer of the Faithful, in ministering to the priest, in preparing the altar and serving the celebration of the Sacrifice, in distributing the Eucharist to the faithful, especially under the species of wine, and sometimes in giving directions regarding the people's gestures and posture (GI, no. 94).

Yet the deacon's ministry at the Eucharist begins well before the opening music does: he should "prepare the sacrifice" (as the bishop's homily in the ordination rite exhorts); thus he should assume the important role of major-domo for the assembly's festive meal. Making sure that the necessary liturgical books, vessels, and vestments are in order will help minimize the last-minute fussing that distracts the assembly and the tension that jeopardizes the effective service of the priest and other ministers. And after preparing for the banquet by fussing with details (like Martha), the deacon should briefly pray and reflect (like Mary)—ideally with the priest and other ministers. (See p. 91 for "Prayer before Ministering at the Eucharist.")

Introductory Rites

The Introductory Rites, which precede the Liturgy of the Word, are the liturgical vestibule through which the deacon and his fellow worshipers enter into the entire eucharistic celebration. "After the people have assembled, the priest and the ministers go to the altar while the entrance song is being sung" (The Order of Mass = OM). In a sense the liturgy begins when the worshipers assemble, not when the priest, deacon, and other ministers process to the sanctuary. Yet the procession should express the conviction of these ministers that they are serving at the mandate of *this* assembly, *this* manifestation of the local church. The entrance procession is a visible means of providing unity and focus for the entire assembly, just as the entrance song is: a blending and uniting of the worshipers' (including the ministers') hearts, minds, and voices as they begin a communal celebration. Neither the procession nor the song is a greeting given to the priest, in spite of how commentators and cantors sometimes announce them.

In the entrance procession the deacon should walk ahead of the servers, readers, and priest, carrying the gospel book high enough so that it can be seen by all. If this symbol of Christ is carried at the head of the entrance procession, the processional cross should be omitted to avoid a duplication of symbols. If incense is to be used in the entrance procession, the censer-bearer should go ahead of the deacon and the gospel book, gently swinging the smoking censer from side to side, or forwards and backwards (depending on the width of the aisle). If the deacon does not carry the gospel book, he walks at the side of the priest (preferably right side).

"On reaching the altar, the priest and ministers make a profound bow" (GI, no. 122). A "profound bow" is a deep bow from the waist; no genuflection is necessary unless the tabernacle is on the axis of processional movement toward the altar (for example, immediately behind the altar); no genuflection is necessary where the tabernacle is off to one side of the church.

According to the rubrics, the deacon and the priest bow upon reaching the altar; yet if the deacon is carrying the gospel book, he omits bowing to the altar (another symbol of Christ) and stands reverently at the altar step while the priest and other ministers bow. After placing the book on the altar (in a place so as to facilitate taking it later during the gospel procession), the deacon and the priest kiss the altar together. This intimate gesture of respect for the holy table should be performed slowly and reverently. If the priest and deacon face the assembly while kissing the altar, they should briefly establish eye contact with them before and after doing so.

The altar may be incensed at this time; if so, the deacon assists the priest by giving him the censer. It has been customary to incense a free-standing altar by starting at the back and walking counterclockwise around it. In the Middle Ages the deacon probably had to raise the chasuble (usually made of heavy fabrics) from the priest's arm so that the latter wouldn't set himself on fire. Today, however, this may be rendered unnecessary by lightweight vestments, and it may actually constrict the priest's swinging the censer. But the deacon should still accompany him as he incenses the altar, joining what may be regarded as a semi-formal procession of two. He should be ready to serve as a fire-fighter should blazing coals fly out of the censer.

In the pre-Vatican II liturgy, the priest and ministers had to genuflect every time they passed the tabernacle, and that meant *many* times. The General Instruction of the Roman Missal (2002) states that if "the tabernacle with the Most Blessed Sacrament is present in the sanctuary, the priest, deacon, and the other ministers genuflect when they approach the altar and when they depart from it, but not during the celebration of Mass itself" (no. 274).

The priest's and the deacon's arrival at their chairs in the sanctuary marks the end of the entrance procession. The deacon customarily sits at the priest's right, but he should sit where he might assist the priest most effectively; both chairs should face the assembly.

The sign of the cross that accompanies the priest's first words is a familiar beginning to public prayer. Yet familiarity with this gesture has sometimes led to a certain sloppiness in doing it, which is especially unbecoming to highly visible liturgical ministers. Romano Guardini exhorts us:

> When we cross ourselves, let it be with a real sign of the cross. Instead of a small cramped gesture that gives no notion of its meaning, let us make a large, unhurried sign, from forehead to breast, from shoulder to shoulder, consciously feeling how it includes the whole of us, our thoughts, our attitudes, our body and soul, every part of us, at once, how it consecrates and sanctifies us.[32]

After the sign of the cross, the priest greets those who have gathered in the Lord's house. This greeting serves to intensify the Lord's presence and the assembly's cohesiveness formed during the entrance procession. The deacon's role during the sign of the cross and the greeting is to make this sacred gesture and give a wholehearted response with the other worshipers—something not possible if he is fumbling with worship leaflets or frantically turning pages in the Roman Missal. Except when performing some assistance, the deacon should keep his hands joined, fingers interlocking or palm-to-palm (he might follow the priest's preference); he should keep his hands high up on his chest.

"The priest, deacon, or other suitable minister may very briefly introduce the Mass of the day" (OM). These *very brief* words of introduction help the assembled worshipers to focus their hearts and minds on this *particular* celebration—*this* feast, season, or occasion. While the priest usually gives this introduction, another minister (for example, the deacon or commentator) may do so. While there is nothing particularly diaconal about introducing the day's celebration, speaking these words might help to establish the necessary bond between the deacon

32. Romano Guardini, *Sacred Signs*, trans. Grace Branham (Wilmington: Michael Glazer Inc., 1979) 13.

and the assembly early in the liturgy. Thus, the deacon should listen attentively to the priest's words or else speak some brief, carefully prepared ones of his own. It is not a time for mini-homilies on the "theme" of the Mass or sneak-previews of the Scripture readings, nor a moment to give away the fire of the homily. Words like "Let us prepare ourselves to celebrate" are inappropriate because the assembly *already* began to celebrate as it gathered (and were the entrance procession and accompanying music, sign of the cross, and greeting all to no purpose?).

The introduction is followed by the penitential rite, for which the Roman Missal includes three forms. The priest invites all to acknowledge their sinfulness and their confidence in God's forgiveness—not to make a detailed examination of conscience.

The third form of the penitential rite (C) has been greatly misunderstood. After the priest invites the assembly to "recall their sins and to repent of them in silence" (OM), either he "or another suitable minister" (for example, the deacon) speaks a series of three invocations addressed to Christ. The Roman Missal's first example is as follows:

> You were sent to heal the contrite:
> Lord, have mercy.
>
> You came to call sinners:
> Christ, have mercy.
>
> You plead for us at the right hand of the Father:
> Lord, have mercy.

Form C of the penitential rite is not a communal confession of faults, but a series of invocations by which the assembly confesses (actually *professes*) their trust in Christ's power to save them from sin; it is not verbalized public soul-searching or a communal examination of conscience (for example, "For the times we failed to be the loving persons you want us to be: Lord, have mercy").

Eight samples of penitential rite C are provided in the Roman Missal, some of which seem especially fitting for particular liturgical seasons. But provision is made for welcome flexibility: other invocations may be composed for a particular feast, season, or occasion. Those provided in the Roman Missal can serve as helpful models for others more tailored to particular congregations and celebrations. Since it is fitting for the deacon to announce these invocations, it might be good for him to compose a set for each Sunday and feast-day Eucharist. These should be addressed to Christ, be theologically correct, and be well-phrased. During Advent and Lent, the deacon (or a cantor) might sing them and the assembly might sing the response. After the priest introduces the penitential rite, the deacon should give the assembly a sufficient amount of time for reflection (a half minute or longer) before beginning the invocations. If the congregation kneels for the rite during times of penitence, the deacon and the priest should also kneel until the priest's absolution is ended by the people's "Amen!"; then all should stand for the opening prayer that follows the penitential rite. If the priest chooses to speak the entire rite, the deacon should enter into it fully and respond with the assembly.

The rite of blessing and sprinkling holy water may fittingly replace the penitential rite on some feasts (for example, the Baptism of the Lord) and during some seasons (for example, on the Sundays of the Easter season). This rite is not a penitential act like the pre-Vatican II *Asperges*; rather, it is a joyful memorial of the baptism that gives admission to the eucharistic banquet. The deacon should assist the priest as he blesses the water (at the chair or elsewhere in the sanctuary). A server might hold the Roman Missal with the text of the blessing; the deacon might hold up the vessel of water during the blessing and carry it through the church as the priest sprinkles the assembly. If the assembly is sufficiently large or spread out to warrant it, the deacon also might sprinkle them (although the rubrics are silent about this). If the priest needs to dry his hands after the sprinkling, the deacon should present a towel.

The "Glory to God" is to be said or sung (preferably sung) on Sundays (except during Advent and Lent), solemnities, feasts, and in solemn celebrations of the local church (for example, ordinations). The deacon might be asked to intone it (depending on musical ability), but in any case he should join the assembly in singing or saying this hymn with the enthusiasm that it deserves.

After the penitential rite (or after the "Glory to God" when prescribed), there follows the opening prayer. This first "presidential" prayer (that is, spoken by the priest) is introduced by: "Let us pray." He does not say: "Let *me* pray." The opening prayer (and the other presidential prayers as well) is essentially a communal prayer that the priest speaks for all and in the name of all. After the assembly has prayed silently in response to the priest's invitation, he gathers their individual prayers into one that he sings or says in the name of all. The assembly voices its "Amen!" to express its concurrence in this prayer and to make this entire prayer its own.

The deacon should receive the priest's invitation to prayer as a personal one to him and to every member of the assembly and respond to it by silent prayer. This is not a time for fussing with worship leaflets or double-checking to see that the correct page for the opening prayer is in place. The deacon or a server holds the Roman Missal for the priest only when he is ready to pray the opening prayer after the silence. The minister should take the bottom of the book in both hands and lean the top against the upper part of the chest, adjusting it if necessary so that the priest can read from it easily. The deacon stands where it is easy for the priest to extend his hands widely and for as many people as possible to see him. He listens attentively to the opening prayer, prays it with those who worship with him, and makes it his own by a strong "Amen!" Then all sit for the Liturgy of the Word.

Liturgy of the Word

"The main part of the Liturgy of the Word is made up of the readings from Sacred Scripture together with the chants occurring between them. The homily, Profession of Faith, and Prayer of the Faithful, however, develop and conclude this part of the Mass" (GI no. 55). The Liturgy of the Word is not a second-rate prelude or elaborate preparation for the Liturgy of the Eucharist. The Scripture readings and the homily based on them are not merely preparatory for receiving Christ in Holy Communion. The Second Vatican Council's Constitution on the Sacred Liturgy affirmed that Christ "is present in his Word, since it is he himself who speaks when the holy Scriptures are read in the Church" (no. 7). The Liturgy of the Word and the Liturgy of the Eucharist form two connected and complementary parts of one celebration, one act of worship.

That is why the entire assembly—including the priest, deacon, and other ministers—should listen attentively to the readings, reflect on them in silence, voice a hearty response in the psalm refrain, and acknowledge their message with an enthusiastic "Thanks be to God!" During the readings the assembly's focus rightfully shifts to the lectern: through the reader who proclaims God's Word there, God speaks divine words to human hearts. Thus the reader deserves (demands!) the assembly's full attention, nothing less. Fussing with books and leaflets, whispering directions to the priest or other ministers, and causing other unnecessary distractions that pull the assembly's attention to the presider's chair, are always to be kept to a minimum—but they are totally out of place during the proclamation of the Scriptures. Luther Reed reminds us that

> in all his public ministrations the minister occupies a conspicuous position. His conduct profoundly affects the worshippers. His attitude throughout should be one of devotion and spiritual concentration. Inattention, fussy rearrangement of notes or announcements, conversation, careless crossing of legs, adjustments of vestments, or too evident scrutiny of the congregation—these are false notes which produce liturgical discord.[33]

33. Luther D. Reed, *Worship: A Study of Corporate Devotion* (Philadelphia: Muhlenberg Press, 1959) 290.

A good general rule for all ministers is: listen when the assembly is listening; respond when the assembly is responding; sing when the assembly is singing; reflect when the assembly is reflecting. Even so, the deacon should be ready to help the reader find the day's readings in the Lectionary if he or she has difficulty doing so, but in an inconspicuous way (this assumes that the deacon knows where they are located). If something should fall to the floor (for example, homily notes or a banner), he should use the natural breaks in the liturgy (for example, after the opening prayer and before the first reading, during the preparation of the gifts) to remove what could later be a hazard to movement in the sanctuary.

On solemn occasions (for example, a liturgy in the cathedral), the deacon might be asked to escort the readers from their seats in the assembly to the lectern, and back again. The deacon goes to where they are seated, stops before them, waits for them to stand and leave their seats, and then walks at their side, bows to the altar with them, and proceeds to the lectern. He stands a little behind them while they read and then accompanies them back to their seats. He waits until they are seated and returns to his chair.

The gospel acclamation, consisting of the alleluia (or another acclamation in Lent) and an appropriate verse, is anticipatory to the proclamation of the gospel (it is not a response to the second reading). The acclamation prepares the assembly to hear Christ speaking to them the words of everlasting life.

"The reading of the Gospel is the high point of the Liturgy of the Word. The Liturgy itself teaches that great reverence is to be shown to it by setting it off from the other readings with special marks of honor" (GI, no. 60). The minister "appointed to proclaim it, . . . prepares himself by a blessing or prayer; . . . ." (*Ibid.*). Only a deacon (or in his absence, a priest) may read the gospel; the deacon (not the priest or a special homilist) is the "first choice" for doing so. This special diaconal role is very ancient; St. Jerome witnesses to this practice late in the fourth century, and from the time of Gregory the Great (d. 604), deacons read only the gospel lesson at the Eucharist. The deacon is to read the gospel and prepare the altar and gifts even if concelebrants are present.

The unique dignity of the gospel led the Church to prepare an evangeliary, or gospel book, which contains the gospel readings for Sundays and feasts. Such a book highlights the proclamation of the gospel and the deacon's role in it. This book, when carried by the deacon at the head of the entrance procession and placed on the altar, needs to get to the lectern for the gospel reading. The gospel procession is a functional transfer of the gospel book from altar to lectern that has been enhanced by powerful symbolic and ritual elements: lighted candles and fragrant incense are two ancient ways to honor Christ present in his Word.

"If incense is used, the deacon assists the priest when he puts incense in the thurible during the singing of the *Alleluia* or other chant. Then he makes a profound bow before the priest and asks for the blessing, saying in a low voice; "*Father, give me your blessing*" (GI, no. 175). The custom of the deacon's asking a blessing from the priest before reading the gospel is as old as the seventh century in Rome. This blessing fulfills a very understandable human need to prepare oneself for important tasks by asking God's blessing; yet this exchange between the deacon and the priest should not call a lot of attention to itself. It should help the deacon focus on the important task of proclaiming the gospel, but it should not distract the assembly from acclaiming the gospel (which is what they should be doing while the deacon receives the blessing from the priest); thus the blessing should overlap the gospel acclamation and not be deferred until it is over.

As all stand to acclaim the gospel (occasionally the deacon may have to invite the assembly to stand if they are slow to do so), the deacon bows before the priest and asks for the blessing. The priest might lay his hand on the deacon's head (an ancient gesture of blessing) as he prays the first part of the prayer: "The Lord be in your heart and on your lips that you may worthily proclaim his gospel." As the priest says, "In the name of the Father, and of the Son, and of the Holy Spirit" and makes the sign of the cross, the deacon signs himself and responds "Amen." Some priests do not know the text of this blessing by heart and substitute the text of the final blessing at Mass. The deacon should ask the priest to learn the proper text provided in the Roman Missal or suggest that he speak one of his own making. The deacon should time his movement to the lectern so that he arrives as the gospel acclamation is ending. If the acclamation ends early, he continues the processional movement and reverently opens the gospel book at the lectern as usual. He should never rush or hurry; silence here is awkward only if he makes it so.

The procession to the lectern should form at the presider's chair. After the priest places incense in the censer and gives the deacon the blessing, the censerbearer leads the procession, followed by two candlebearers, and, lastly, the deacon. If the sanctuary is small and crowded, the candlebearers should walk as a pair ahead of the deacon; if the sanctuary is large and ample, they should flank him. All process to the front of the altar and line up in this way:

When all have stopped before the altar, only the deacon should bow; he goes to the altar, takes the gospel book and holds it high, turns to face the assembly, and waits until the servers resume the procession to the lectern. He then carries the book behind them. The censerbearer steps to the rear of the lectern; the candlebearers stand on either side of it (facing each other) if there is sufficient space, but behind it (side-by-side) if there isn't. The deacon places the gospel book on the lectern, opens it to the proper page, and stands with hands joined while singing the gospel acclamation with the assembly.

If the altar in the church is elevated a number of steps (usually three) above the sanctuary floor, a modification in this suggested gospel procession is necessary. After taking the gospel book, the deacon returns to the sanctuary floor, turns toward the lectern with the servers, and waits for the candlebearer behind him to come around in front and pair up with the other candlebearer. Then the procession resumes as indicated above.

If the presider's chair is placed behind the altar, the gospel procession might be arranged as follows. When the gospel acclamation is begun, two servers take their processional candles and line up with the corners of the altar (facing it):

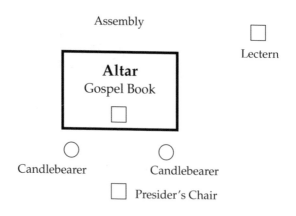

At the same time, two servers leave the sacristy with censer and boat and go to the priest at his chair, where he places incense. Then these two servers line up behind the candlebearers:

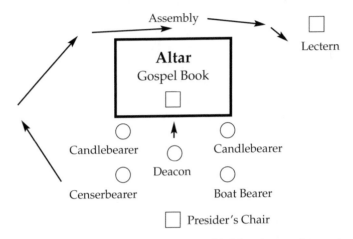

Assembly

Lectern

Altar

Gospel Book

Candlebearer

Candlebearer

Deacon

Censerbearer

Boat Bearer

Presider's Chair

All wait while the deacon receives his blessing and goes to the altar between the two rows of servers. After he takes the gospel book from the altar and raises it high, he turns to his left, and the servers turn and move as a group to their left, across the front of the sanctuary to the lectern. The deacon comes last in this procession, but he might also walk in the middle of the servers. The reading of the gospel at the lectern takes place as described above. This pattern can be adapted to particular worship spaces.

Gabe Huck well expresses the sentiments that should be the deacon's during the entrance and gospel processions:

> The dance is rigid down the aisle, a book embraced, held high, held dear: the common carrier of the tales on fiber come from cotton fields and pulp from forest cut in Maine. What earth has given hands have made flat, thin and bound between two boards, the pages covered now with marks that image sounds that image all: the pictures of pictures only are letters gathered into words and words lined up and bundled, tied—yet here's the kernel of ourselves: the poems, genealogies, laws, letters,

> sayings, prophesies, psalms, stories, visions handed on from
> mouth to mouth and tongue to tongue and page to page: a year
> or three to tell it round again, this book that dances now in in-
> cense sweet and sweet its alphabet to kiss.[34]

Proclaiming the gospel from such a noble book calls for previous preparation. The deacon should look up the pronunciation of unfamiliar words and practice the reading in advance
and out loud. He should mark the page with a ribbon or cloth
bookmark (scraps of old bulletins or scratch paper are aesthetically displeasing and unworthy of the contents of the book). He
should know the order and arrangement of the gospel book so
well as not to be embarrassed by the inability to find the reading should the ribbon get moved or the bookmark fall out (for
example, to avoid fumbling for the Christmas Midnight Mass
gospel at the back of the book he should note that it is near the
front). He should know the opening dialogue by heart in order
to maintain welcome eye contact with the assembly throughout; this will help draw them into the proclamation. He should
also know by heart the name of the evangelist who wrote the
text, so that he won't have to look down awkwardly at the
book after saying, "A reading from the holy Gospel according
to _____." While the assembly responds, "Glory to you,
Lord," with the right thumb the deacon makes a small sign of
the cross on the opening word of the day's gospel and then
does the same on the forehead, lips, and chest (perhaps more
significantly, on the heart). When the assembly has finished its
response, he proceeds to honor the book with incense: three
double swings of the censer (center, left, right) toward the book
seem fitting; but no matter how the incensing is done (with vig-
orous swinging or restrained "clinking the chain"), it should be
significant (not perfunctory or minimal) and graceful (not hur-
ried or sloppy). He takes the book in his hands and holds it for
the reading. At the end he pauses for a few seconds before
looking at the assembly and saying, "The Gospel of the Lord."

34. Gabe Huck, "Book," in *Assembly*, vol. 8, no. 1 (September 1981) 139.

The rubrics are silent about lifting up the book and "presenting" it to the assembly before saying these words. Such lifting up of the book may serve to unduly emphasize the gospel as printed text rather than as proclaimed Word.

After the assembly has responded, "Praise to you, Lord Jesus Christ," the deacon kisses the book while saying quietly (that is, silently): "May the words of the gospel wipe away our sins." This tender gesture is a mark of reverence for Christ who speaks in the gospel. In eighth-century Rome, all the clergy present kissed the book after the gospel was proclaimed. A remnant of this ancient practice may be the custom at episcopal liturgies whereby the deacon presents the gospel book to the bishop so that he can kiss the page just read from. (At an episcopal liturgy the deacon should consult the master of ceremonies about this custom.)

After the gospel reading, the censerbearer takes the censer to the sacristy by the most direct route; the candlebearers pair up and return their candles to the place where they got them. If the deacon does not preach, he returns to the chair by following the candlebearers or by walking between them, depending on the amount of space in the sanctuary. But if there is to be no homily or profession of faith, he may remain at the lectern for the general intercessions (GI, no. 177).

The homily and profession of faith normally follow the proclamation of the gospel on Sundays and holy days. "Not only social action ministry but also teaching are integral parts of diaconal ministry in the faith community. As a consequence of this teaching mandate, the deacon may appropriately preach in liturgical celebrations."[35] The deacon exercises the ministry of preaching (as well as the ministry of presiding at baptisms, marriages, and funerals) according to the authorization received from the bishop and diocesan norms.

Reverence for the gospel book should extend beyond reading from it. Thus the deacon either leaves the book open on the

---

35. Robert W. Hovda, "For Deacons," *Touchstones for Liturgical Ministers*, 18.

lectern and places his homily notes neatly on top of it (this procedure can underscore the idea of "breaking open" the Word of God in both the proclamation of the gospel and the homily), or he closes the book reverently and places his homily notes neatly beside it. The gospel book should not be relegated to a chair or side table after the reading.

If the priest is to preach, the deacon bows to the altar with him as he goes to the lectern and as the deacon returns to his chair. He remains standing until the priest reaches the lectern. The deacon stands when the priest returns from the lectern and sits when he does. This is customary etiquette for all similar situations, not just at Mass. The Creed, if it is to follow the homily, should call forth the deacon's attentive participation as he professes his faith with the assembly.

The general intercessions (prayer of the faithful) conclude the Liturgy of the Word. In these prayers the deacon helps the assembly exercise its priestly role and privilege of interceding for the needs of the whole world; his voice becomes the assembly's voice. The deacon's ministry inside and outside the liturgy makes him the logical minister to lead these prayers, as *Study Text VI* explains:

> Making intercession in the name of the assembly has traditionally been a diaconal role because it is the deacon, serving among the people in a ministry of charity, who ought to know well the needs of the community. He can give voice to those needs. The deacon, therefore, has an intercessory function within the eucharist, and in any liturgy in which intercessions and litanies figure. In a sense the general intercessions are the prototype of diaconal prayer.[36]

The priest introduces the general intercessions at the chair by making an opening invitation to prayer; the deacon announces the intentions at the ambo (lectern) (GI, no. 177). This is the deacon's normal, ordinary function, but if the intentions are to be sung and he does not believe his musical ability is a

36. *Study Text* VI, 40.

match for them, he might defer to a cantor. He could remain at his chair and announce the intentions from the priest's microphone (functioning alongside each other would serve to unify the prayer by providing a single focus).

The deacon may be called upon to write the general intercessions as well as to lead them. Robert Hovda correctly observes that

> assistance in the preparation as well as the actual proclaiming of the community's general intercessions is an appropriate diaconal function. . . . Needless to say, the general intercessions should reflect sufferings and needs broader than those of the local church—the entire church and world, in fact—but local needs are an essential part. A functioning deacon should be more aware of those local needs than anyone in the area.[37]

Some helpful resources for preparing these prayers are the sample formulas at the back of the Roman Missal; statement of the Bishops' Committee on the Liturgy entitled *General Intercessions* (Washington: United States Catholic Conference, 1979); Robert Hovda's article, "The Prayer of General Intercession," *Worship* 44 (October 1970) 497–502; and Michael Kwatera, O.S.B., *Preparing the General Intercessions* (Collegeville: Liturgical Press, 1996). The General Instruction indicates that "as a rule, the series of intentions is to be: a. For the needs of the Church; b. For public authorities and the salvation of the world; c. For those burdened by any kind of difficulty; d. For the local community" (GI, no. 70).

"Nevertheless, in a particular celebration, such as Confirmation, Marriage, or a Funeral, the series of intentions may reflect more closely the particular occasion" (no. 70). The United States' bishops have suggested that "there always be a petition for peace in the general intercessions at every eucharistic celebration."[38]

37. Hovda, "For Deacons," 18.
38. *The Challenge of Peace: God's Promise and Our Response* (Washington: United States Catholic Conference, 1983) no. 295, 90.

The deacon's service in the Liturgy of the Word, both in proclaiming the gospel and leading the general intercessions, should reveal him as messenger and bearer of good news to the poor, as servant and intercessor in the image of Christ.

Liturgy of the Eucharist

"When the Prayer of the Faithful is completed, all sit, and the Offertory chant begins. . . . The acolyte or other lay minister arranges the corporal, the purificator, the chalice, the pall, and the Missal upon the altar" (GI, no. 139). Although other ministers may assist in this task, it is the deacon's function to ensure that the necessary vessels and other objects are placed on the altar and to assist the priest in receiving the assembly's gifts. Concelebrating priests may not assume these and other diaconal functions when a deacon is present.

The corporal might be placed on the altar before Mass begins; then the altar fittingly could receive the gifts of bread and wine *before* it receives the Roman Missal, microphone, etc., since the gifts are the important symbols of the assembly's self-offering with Christ in the Eucharist. If incense is used at the preparation of the altar and gifts, the Roman Missal and microphone should not be placed on the altar until after the incensing. Before Mass the deacon should check with the priest to see where he wants the Roman Missal placed for easiest reading so that as the deacon arranges the gifts room can be left for it. The deacon opens the Roman Missal to the priest's prayers that begin "Blessed are you, Lord, God of all creation." Such attention to practical matters will minimize fussing to rearrange plates of bread, chalice, Roman Missal, etc. The deacon should know where each object should be placed, place it there, and leave it there.

When everything is ready, the deacon nods to the priest as a signal for him to approach the altar or goes to his chair and accompanies him to the altar. It is aesthetically more pleasing to approach and leave the altar from the center than by diagonal shortcuts. He hands the paten or plate of bread to the priest for the prayer "Blessed are you, Lord, God of all creation." The preparation of the chalice takes place either at the altar or a side table. The deacon prepares the chalice by pouring wine and a little water into it. In pouring the water, he says silently: "By the mystery of this water and wine may we come to share in the divinity of Christ, who humbled himself to share in our humanity." He hands the chalice to the priest for the prayer "Blessed are you." If incense is used, he assists the priest by opening the incense boat, taking the censer from the censer-bearer, and giving it to the priest, who will incense the gifts, cross, and altar (starting at the back and walking counterclockwise around it). After accompanying the priest around the altar, the deacon (or another minister) should incense him (perhaps with three double swings of the censer), the ministers, and the rest of the assembly; for incensing the latter, the deacon might move up and down the aisles, swinging the censer toward the people. It is good to practice with the censer.

After assisting the priest in washing his hands (unless a server is to do this), the deacon moves to the position where he can be most helpful to the priest during the Eucharistic Prayer: either close to the left side of the priest if the deacon is to assist with the Roman Missal or a little behind and off to the right side. He should turn pages unobtrusively (unlike the deacon who reportedly reaches *over* the priest's extended arms to do so). He should remember that a deacon is not glued to one spot; he should move anywhere there is need for his assistance. Concelebrants should remain out of the deacon's way when he ministers at the altar (GI, no. 215).

"From the epiclesis until the priest shows the chalice, the deacon normally remains kneeling" (GI, no. 179). But a deacon's age or physical condition may make this difficult or impossible for him to do. In this case, he should remain standing.

If standing, after the words of institution (the Lord's words at the Last Supper), the deacon makes a profound bow when the priest genuflects. The deacon does not say "Let us proclaim the mystery of faith," because these words, as part of the Eucharistic Prayer, belong to the priest.

At the doxology which concludes the Eucharistic Prayer, the deacon stands beside the priest and lifts up the cup as the priest lifts up the bread (concelebrants should not lift up other cups and plates). Because the doxology is part of the Eucharistic Prayer, only the priest (and concelebrants) should sing or say it. Both the priest and deacon should keep the gifts raised until the assembly has responded "Amen!" Replacing the gifts on the altar before the "Amen!" is to render the ending of the Eucharistic Prayer anticlimactic and to rob this final tribute of glory and honor to the Father of its meaning. Turning the pages in the Roman Missal should never overlap the doxology and "Amen!" but the deacon must know where the Communion Rite is found in the Roman Missal so that it can be easily located during the fitting pause between the "Amen!" and the invitation to the Lord's Prayer.

Communion Rite

After the Lord's Prayer and the prayer "Deliver us, Lord, from every evil," the priest says the prayer for peace. Immediately after it, he extends his hands, embracing the assembly as it were, as he gives the greeting: "The peace of the Lord be with you always." When the assembly has answered, "And also with you," the deacon invites them to share in a ritual gesture that seals their unity in the peace of Christ: "Let us offer each other the sign of peace." "Sign" is a richly ambiguous word for which "handshake" should not be substituted; "sign" invites husbands and wives to exchange a genuine kiss; close friends, a hug or embrace; strangers, a polite but sincere handshake. Yet the deacon might adapt this invitation to the feast, season, or occasion, taking care that his words are few (this is not a time for an extensive discourse on how blessed peacemakers are or on what a great thing peace is). The priest should give the deacon and other ministers the sign of peace; since the priest and deacon cannot conveniently share it with all present, sharing it with other ministers in the sanctuary is really a vicarious gesture in which the entire assembly shares: part receive for the whole. What should be avoided is giving the false impression that the peace of Christ must come from priest to deacon to ministers to people in the pew; all the members of the assembly, holy and priestly, can and must share the sign of peace quite apart from any clerical authorization or empowerment to do so.

The breaking of bread follows the sign of peace, during which the deacon may assist the priest in breaking the bread and placing it in the Communion vessels. If it is necessary to bring additional bread from the tabernacle to the altar (this rarely should be the case), the deacon should do so before the priest says, "This is the Lamb of God. . . ." This will help to make the priest's words and gestures more inclusive: all the eucharistic food on the altar at this moment is the banquet. If concelebrants are present, the deacon might bring the bread to them so that they can hold a piece of it during the priest's words, "This is the Lamb of God." After the priest's Communion, "the deacon receives Communion under both kinds from the priest himself and then assists the priest in distributing Communion to the people. If Communion is given under both kinds, the deacon himself administers the chalice to the communicants" (GI, no. 182). "Neither deacons nor lay ministers may ever receive Holy Communion in the manner of a concelebrating priest" (*Norms for the Distribution and Reception of Holy Communion under Both Kinds in the Dioceses of the United States*, no. 39).

Where the Communion of a large number of ministers may become lengthy, "the presider could minister to the deacon and/or to two communion ministers. Then they in turn could minister to the others so that the communion of the assembly may begin without delay."[39] The Norms indicate that the

---

39. Michael Ahlstrom, in *Liturgy 80*, vol. 14, no. 1 (January–February 1983) 12.

priest, deacon, and extraordinary ministers are to receive Communion before serving the assembly (no. 39); such a practice reveals the Eucharist to be the nourishing food that strengthens the ministers to serve the assembly. "The deacon may assist the priest in handing the vessels containing the Body and Blood of the Lord to the extraordinary ministers of Holy Communion" (*Norms*, no. 40). Some helpful suggestions for ministering the Body and Blood of Christ are contained in the Liturgical Press booklet *The Ministry of Communion*. If there are a sufficient number of Communion ministers, the deacon might choose to forego ministering the cup so as to oversee the sharing of Communion; if so, he brings extra bread and wine to the ministers and ensures that all goes smoothly. Such service for the sake of hospitality and good order can minimize unwarranted delays or confusion in the sharing of Communion.

When Communion is finished, collecting the unused bread and wine may be done at the altar or side table. The deacon consumes any remaining fragments or gathers the unused bread into containers for placement in the tabernacle, the transfer to which can be done by an extraordinary minister of Holy Communion. The unused wine is consolidated into as few cups as possible and taken to the sacristy. The deacon might assume the responsibility of inviting the ministers to consume the remaining bread and wine after Communion or after Mass. If the amount of bread and wine is such that the deacon can consume it easily and inconspicuously, he might do so and then wash the chalice and other vessels at the side table; "but it is also permissible to leave the vessels that need to be purified, suitably covered at the credence table on a corporal, and to purify them immediately after Mass following the dismissal of the people" (GI, no. 183).

Crumbs should be disposed of reverently after each Mass, either by consuming them or by mixing them with water and drinking the mixture or pouring it into the sacrarium. If the deacon cleanses the paten or plates during Mass, wiping the crumbs from them into the chalice is the ordinary and sufficient means of doing so. "The purification of the chalice is done with water alone or with wine and water, which is then drunk by whoever does the purification" (GI, no. 279). It is preferable that all Communion vessels be cleansed in the sacristy after the liturgy.

Concluding Rite

After the unused bread and wine have been reverently removed from the altar, the deacon returns to his chair. A few moments of silent reflection are welcome here, especially for ministers who have been busy during Communion. Fussing with worship leaflets, lists of announcements, or the Roman Missal is not conducive to the deacon's or assembly's thanksgiving for the gift of the Lord's Body and Blood in Communion.

After a period of silence (or psalm or song of praise), the priest sings or says the prayer after Communion. The deacon assists with the Roman Missal as for the opening prayer (unless a server is to do this). "Once the prayer after Communion has been said, the deacon makes brief announcements to the people, if indeed any need to be made unless the priest prefers to do this himself" (GI, no. 184). Because the deacon's ministry may put him in a good (perhaps the best) position to know particular persons and intentions for which the assembly should pray, it is fitting for him to announce such things as illnesses, funerals, and marriages of parishioners; also, he might mention opportunities for bodily and spiritual assistance that are available to the people. These announcements should not be made from the lectern where the Scripture readings were proclaimed.

On certain feasts and occasions the priest may conclude the Eucharist with a solemn blessing or prayer over the people. He greets the assembly, "The Lord be with you," and they respond, "And also with you." Then the deacon, with hands joined or extended in invitation, addresses a formal but non-demanding request to the assembly: "Bow your heads and pray for God's blessing." After all have briefly prayed in silence, the priest speaks the solemn blessing or prayer over the people, concluding with the Trinitarian blessing and the sign of the cross. The deacon and the assembly have the last words: his dismissal, followed by their response, sends each member "out to do good works, praising and blessing God" (GI, no. 90c). This is not a moment for replaying the "theme" of the Mass or the homily; rather, it is a moment for exhorting the assembly to renew their efforts to love and serve the Lord in the members of his Body. The dismissal echoes the diaconal call to serve God and God's people, especially the poorest and weakest of them. Thus diaconal ministry within the liturgy returns the deacon and the assembly to ministry outside it.

As the exit procession forms, the deacon ordinarily kisses the altar with the priest, makes the customary reverence to the altar (a profound bow) and leaves the sanctuary in the same order as at the beginning of Mass (but without the gospel book).

Initiation of Adults

The Rite of Christian Initiation of Adults (= RCIA, 1972) reflects ancient and contemporary awareness that adult growth in faith leading to initiation is a process fittingly marked by stages. Deacons may serve the Church and those preparing to enter it through the ministry of evangelizing, catechizing, ascertaining the readiness of candidates for initiation, and celebrating the rites throughout the process at Easter and during the Easter season. The introduction to the RCIA highlights the deacon's role in the stages of preparation and celebration: "Deacons who are available should be ready to help. If the Episcopal Conference judges it opportune to have permanent deacons, it should make provision that their number is adequate to permit the stages, periods, and exercises of the catechumenate to take place everywhere when required by pastoral needs" (no. 47).

The first period is *evangelization* (precatechumenate), during which deacons may assist priests and catechists in explaining the Gospel of Jesus Christ to all who seek to know more about it (no. 11). The nascent faith of these inquirers must be nourished by prayer; thus, "During the period of the precatechumenate, pastors should help the inquirers with suitable prayers" (no. 13). The deacon's familiarity with and love for various kinds of prayer (public and private, set and free) will do much to help the inquirers learn how to pray.

The deacon's role in the second period, the *catechumenate*, is both catechetical and liturgical. The deacon's catechesis of the inquirers should enable him to help the pastor judge whether they have outwardly manifested the inner dispositions needed to enter the catechumenate, "an extended period during which the candidates are given pastoral formation and are trained by suitable discipline" (no. 19). Throughout this period, the deacon may preside at celebrations of the Word, by which the catechumens can achieve "a suitable knowledge of dogmas and precepts" and also "an intimate understanding of the mystery of salvation in which they desire to share" (no. 19:1). The diaconal functions may be exercised in such catechumenal rites as the rite of becoming catechumens (nos. 68–97); minor exorcisms (nos. 109–18); blessings of the catechumens (nos. 125–30), including the anointing with the oil of exorcism (no. 130; female adults should be anointed on the hands, not on the chest).

In the rite of becoming catechumens, the deacon himself may preside or assist the priest. At the conclusion of the rite, the deacon should dismiss the catechumens (no. 96); also,

> Ordinarily . . . when they [catechumens] are present in the assembly of the faithful, they should be dismissed in a friendly manner before the eucharistic celebration begins [that is, before the Liturgy of the Eucharist], unless there are difficulties; they must await their baptism which will bring them into the priestly people and allow them to participate in the Christian worship of the new covenant (no. 19:3).

Although dismissing the catechumens is an ancient diaconal function, no text is provided in the rite; care and sensitivity in dismissing them "in a friendly manner" will be appreciated by the entire assembly. A helpful resource is *Sunday Dismissals for the RCIA* by Mary K. Milne, O.S.U. (Collegeville: Liturgical Press, 1993).

The third period, *purification and enlightenment*, usually coincides with the season of Lent. The preparation of candidates for initiation at the approaching Easter Vigil is intensified. Again the deacon's catechetical and liturgical ministry should prepare him to judge the readiness of the candidates for baptism (no. 135) together with the priests, catechists, sponsors, and godparents.

At a liturgical service on the First Sunday of Lent, the deacon may represent these persons who have been responsible for preparing the candidates as he presents the catechumens to the assembly and the bishop (or pastor) for "election" (admission to the sacraments of initiation at the Easter Vigil). After the catechumens have professed their desire to receive these sacraments, they give their names to be enrolled. In many places the names are written by each candidate or clearly pronounced and written by the godparent or by the presider. If this procedure is followed, the deacon might lead the candidates to the book (perhaps placed on the altar) and assist them as they write their names; or he might hold the book and let them approach for the enrollment; or he might take the book to each of them in turn (this might be the most expeditious and yet personal way).

During the rite of enrollment, the deacon should lead the intercessions and litanies for the candidates (no. 148); during the scrutinies on the Third, Fourth, and Fifth Sundays of Lent, he should give necessary directions for bowing or kneeling (nos. 162, 169, 176) and lead the intercessory prayers for the elect (nos. 163, 170, 177). He should also dismiss the elect after the rite of enrollment and the scrutinies (nos. 150, 165, 172, 179) and invite them to come forward to receive the Church's profession of faith and the Lord's Prayer on the days appointed for these presentations (nos. 184–92, especially nos. 186 and 191).

Throughout this period of purification and enlightenment, the deacon may celebrate exorcisms of the elect (no. 156).

The deacon's liturgical ministry during the sacraments of initiation at the Easter Vigil sets a seal on his previous catechetical and liturgical ministry to those who are to be initiated. Knowledgeable assistance to the presider (bishop or priest), as well as to the candidates for initiation, will help ensure the orderly succession of rites during the Easter Vigil. It is a night for the most reverent gestures, most clear directions, and most loving service in welcoming new members of the Body of Christ through baptism, confirmation, and first Eucharist.

During the fourth period, *postbaptismal catechesis (mystagogia)*, the newly baptized acquire a deeper understanding of the paschal mystery into which they have been initiated and upon which they seek to ground their lives more and more. "The main place for the postbaptismal catechesis, or mystagogia will be the Masses for neophytes, that is, the Sunday Masses of the Easter season" (no. 39). The homilist should express the Church's special delight in its newest children as the community seeks to strengthen their commitment. Deacons who preach on the Sundays of Easter should mention the names of the adults initiated at the Vigil and see to it that they have been included in the general intercessions (no. 236).

Baptism of Children

The Rite of Baptism for Children includes the rites and ceremonies by which a deacon solemnly baptizes infants. His liturgical ministry in this sacrament, as in the initiation of adults, will often set the seal on his catechetical ministry begun well in advance of the baptismal day itself. Often he will share the responsibility of pastor and parishioners to help "prepare families for the baptism of their children and to help them in the task of Christian formation they have undertaken"

(Introduction, no. 7:1). His role in preparing parents for the baptism of their children becomes especially significant if he also serves as the presiding minister of the sacrament.

"Everyone who performs the rite of baptism should do so with care and devotion; he must also try to be understanding and friendly to all" (no. 7:2). Here the rite challenges the minister to overcome the frustration that easily arises from the occasional tardiness of parents and sponsors, the sometimes rambunctious behavior of screeching and squirming babies (and their siblings), and a series of ceremonies marked by a fair amount of repetition. A sense of humor may be one of the most important things that the minister brings to the celebration.

The various parts of the rite can be divided between priest and deacon, but not at the cost of fragmenting the unity of the rite or multiplying distractions (of which there will be a sufficient number). If he assists the priest, the deacon might read the Scripture lesson(s), unless someone from the family is to do this, preach, lead the intercessions, and invoke the saints in the brief litany. The priest might be responsible for the prayer of exorcism and the anointing before baptism, as well as the actions at the font (blessing of water, renunciation of sin and profession of faith, baptism and postbaptismal rites). It would be disruptive and distracting to have the priest bless the water, the deacon lead the renunciation and the profession and then baptize, the priest anoint the child with chrism, the deacon present the white garment and lighted candle, the priest conclude the rite by introducing the Lord's Prayer and giving the blessing. Such a shuffling of the presider's role between priest and deacon is arbitrary and distracting, and violates sound liturgical principles; a satisfactory "division of labor" in this sacramental rite should be worked out between them in advance. Certainly the deacon should assist the priest by holding the book, oil, towel, chrism, candle, etc., and presenting them as needed. If the deacon is presiding, someone should assist him in this way.

The introduction to the Rite of Baptism for Children identifies a variety of different ministries and roles in this celebration, including that of parent and presider (see nos. 4–7). A deacon should not preside at the baptism of his own child because this confuses two distinct ministries. The revised Rite of Baptism for Children places great emphasis on the role of the father and mother, both during and after this celebration (see the Introduction, no. 5); thus for a deacon, the ministerial role of parent supersedes that of presider. The local pastor, who more clearly represents the local church which welcomes new members, should be asked to preside in such cases.

When presiding, the deacon should effectively use the options provided in the rite, so that he (perhaps assisted by the parents) can tailor each celebration of baptism to the feast, season, or occasion, yet never forgetting that every baptism celebrates Christ's paschal mystery and a Christian's sharing in it. The baptism of infants on the feast of the Holy Family should "feel" different from baptism on Pentecost Sunday or the Sixteenth Sunday in Ordinary Time. What makes the difference is the choice of Scripture readings, the emphasis in the homily, and the choice of words in explanations and prayers (for example, in the intercessions and blessings at the conclusion of the rite).

The deacon should briefly and clearly explain the various parts of the rite immediately before performing them. This can be done most effectively if he is so thoroughly familiar with the rite that he need not cling to the book as if it were a life preserver. Some spontaneity in introducing the parts of the rite is welcome and refreshing for all participants, including the deacon. His clear and copious directions will make it unnecessary for the parents, godparents, and others present to clutter their hands with booklets. He should invite the assembly to stand or sit or process as necessary, invite the children to sit or stand where they will be able to see easily, and clearly announce the desired response to prayers. For example: "As we ask God to bless this water, which washes us for new life in Christ, please respond in the words: 'Blessed be God forever.'" Clear and copious directions—a form of liturgical hospitality on the deacon's part—will reduce nervousness on the assembly's part.

Addressing the baby, parents, and godparents by name in the texts of the rite will make it more personal.

Some helpful suggestions for the baptism of children:

- Treat the babies as *real persons*. Learn and use their names. Address them face to face; they are not bundles of blankets to be sneaked up on.
- If the assembly is small, invite all present to follow the parents and godparents in making the sign of the cross on the baby's forehead.
- If the babies are carried to a separate place for the duration of the Liturgy of the Word, they should be brought back *before* the intercessions (not *after* this prayer, as in no. 48 of the rite). The assembly is praying for *these* babies, so they should be present. During the parents' baptismal preparation period, help them write some petitions that they can read at this time. The names of the babies' patron saints, as well as the names of the parish patron(s), should be included (if this can be done easily).
- In explaining the Prayer of Exorcism, avoid using the word "exorcism"; it may recall William Blatty's terrifying novel and movie. Invite all present (not just parents and godparents) to take part in the "Renunciation of Evil and Profession of Faith" (nos. 56–59); introduce the two sections with words like "Now let us reject the power of evil" and "Let us now profess our faith," and include an invitation to respond to your questions in the words "I do."
- After the assembly has professed their faith, sprinkle them with the water just blessed, explaining this gesture as a memorial of their own baptism; sprinkling them after the final blessing is an alternative. At the actual baptism, invite the parent who is not holding the baby to place a hand on the child; then invite the godparents to stand behind the parents and place their hands on the parents' shoulders.
- If immersing the baby, grasp the baby firmly before placing it up to the neck in the water, or first ask the mother

to place the baby in the water and then pour a good amount of water over the baby's head. A padded table and fluffy towels should be ready nearby for drying and clothing the baby. If pouring the water rather than immersing the baby, using a cupped hand is preferable to a shell, pitcher, or punch cup.

- In the anointing after baptism, use a generous amount of chrism, the oil marked SC (*Sancta Chrisma*). Anoint the crown of the head (not the forehead, which the bishop anoints at confirmation), being careful not to press down on the baby's softspot. Let the chrism remain on the baby's head.

- At the anointing with chrism and the giving of the white garment and the lighted candle, say the words after doing the actions, allowing the symbols and gestures to speak their message in silence. If the baby has been wearing the white garment throughout the entire service (not an ideal practice), gesture toward it and say, "See in the new white garment you are wearing this day the outward sign of your Christian dignity. . . ." Give the unlighted candles to the fathers or godfathers and then present the lighted Easter Candle to each one so that he can light the baby's candle from it. Invite the parents to light these candles on important days in their children's life of faith: patron saints' days, baptismal anniversaries, first Communion day, confirmation day.

- After these rites ask the assembly to gather around the altar for the Lord's Prayer. The movement to the altar is prescribed in the rite and should not be omitted lightly, since it indicates that the baptism of children will one day lead them to the eucharistic table of the Lord around which we pray his prayer before sharing his Body and Blood. Invite the assembly to join their hands for this prayer.

- During the concluding blessing, lay hands on the mother's head, then on the father's, and lastly extend them over the assembly, thereby matching the gestures to the words of the prayer.

- Conclude the liturgy of baptism with a song, such as "Now Thank We All Our God" or "Praise God, From Whom All Blessings Flow," followed by a sign of peace that seals the assembly's unity in faith and by a kiss that welcomes the baby into the Church.

Reception of Baptized Christians into Full Communion with the Catholic Church

The diaconal ministry of teaching the Christian faith may include preparing baptized members of various Christian Churches or ecclesial communities to become members of the Roman Catholic Church. If so, it is very fitting for the deacon to assist or preside at the liturgical celebration that marks this important moment in their life of faith.

The Foreword and Introduction to the Rite of Reception of Baptized Christians into Full Communion with the Catholic Church explain the significance of the rite and contain suggestions for its celebration. Chapters I and II describe the rite of reception within Mass and outside Mass, respectively. Chapter III lists the Scripture readings that may be chosen for the celebration.

The rite of reception into full communion generally takes place at the Sunday Eucharist. In some personal or family circumstances, the candidate may not wish to be received so publicly; yet the reception should still take place within a Eucharist at which a few members of the local community, friends, and others who have helped the person come into full communion can be present. If for a serious reason the Eucharist cannot be celebrated, the reception takes place during a liturgy of the Word.

If a deacon bears responsibility for the candidate's preparation, it is most fitting that he preach at the Eucharist and preside at the rite of reception. In the homily "the celebrant should express gratitude to God and should speak of baptism as the basis for reception, of confirmation to be received or already received, and of the eucharist to be celebrated for the first time by the newly received Christian" with fellow Roman Catholics (no. 14b). At the end of the homily, the deacon invites the candidate to come forward with his or her sponsor(s) and make the profession of faith (no. 14c). The candidate recites the Nicene Creed with the assembly and affirms adherence to the teachings of the Roman Catholic Church. Then, the deacon lays his right hand on the candidate's head (unless confirmation is to follow), and says the formula of reception (no. 16). If the candidate is to be confirmed, the priest (not the deacon) lays his hands on the candidate's head during the prayer in no. 17. After this prayer, the deacon presents the chrism to the priest, who anoints the candidate on the forehead; then the deacon assists the priest in washing or wiping his hands. Then the priest gives a sign of friendship and acceptance to the newly received person; the deacon and the sponsor(s) should do the same, either at this time or after the general intercessions. If the person is not confirmed during the service, the greeting follows the formula of reception. The deacon might invite the assembly's applause as its way of expressing acceptance and approval of the one received, either after the sign of welcome that follows confirmation or after the general intercessions (no. 20).

"The general intercessions follow the reception (and confirmation). In the introduction, the celebrant should mention baptism, confirmation, and the Eucharist, and express gratitude to God. The one received into full communion is mentioned in the first of the intercessions" (no. 19). Sample intercessions are included in no. 30. After these prayers, the one received returns to his or her place, and Mass continues as usual. "It is fitting that communion be received under both kinds by the one received," by the person's sponsor(s), parents, and spouse (if they are Catholics) and by all Catholics present (no. 21). Thus, the deacon should be prepared to minister the cup or oversee the sharing of Communion.

Chapter II gives directions for the "Rite of Reception Outside Mass." After an appropriate song, a Scripture reading, and a homily based on it, the reception takes place as at Mass (nos. 14c–19). The general intercessions are concluded with the Lord's Prayer (sung or recited by all), and a blessing. Then the sponsor(s)—and, if they are few, the whole assembly—may greet the newly received person at the conclusion of the liturgy.

"The names of those received into full communion should be recorded in a special book, with the date and place of baptism also noted" (no. 13).

Confirmation

As a minister of the gospel and a teacher of the Christian faith, the deacon may share the pastor's responsibility "to see that all the baptized come to the fullness of Christian initiation and are carefully prepared for confirmation" (Rite of Confirmation, no. 3). If he has helped to prepare candidates for this sacrament and has helped plan the liturgy, the deacon's assistance to the bishop during the liturgical celebration will be especially significant to the deacon and to those he has prepared.

Confirmation ordinarily is celebrated within Mass. The deacon should be ready to assist the bishop with his crozier and miter during the entrance (unless someone else is to do this). When the deacon takes or gives the crozier, he should keep the crook (curved part) turned toward him. When he gives the miter or puts it on the bishop, he should turn it upside down and make sure that the lappets (the two strips which hang down) are turned toward himself.

After the deacon reads the gospel, the bishop may expect him to present the gospel book so that the bishop can kiss it;

the deacon should check with the master of ceremonies about this before the liturgy.

After the gospel "the pastor or another priest, deacon or catechist presents the candidates for confirmation, according to the custom of the region" (no. 21). After the bishop extends his hands over the candidates and sings or says a prayer for the gifts of the Holy Spirit, the deacon brings the chrism to the bishop, holding it in such a way that the bishop can easily dip his thumb into it and anoint each candidate on the forehead. The deacon remains at the bishop's side until all the candidates have been confirmed and then removes the chrism. He assists the bishop in washing his hands at his chair by bringing a tray with a bowl of warm, soapy water, a small pitcher of water, quartered lemons, and towels, and then by holding the tray on the bishop's lap (unless servers have been assigned to these tasks).

The deacon might lead the general intercessions which follow, although one of the newly confirmed might do so instead. Either a prescribed solemn blessing or a prayer over the people concludes the Mass, for which the deacon should invite the assembly to bow their heads.

Reconciliation

In the communal rites of reconciliation (forms II and III of the Rite of Penance), the deacon's ministry includes proclaiming the gospel and possibly preaching, exhorting the assembly to penance in the general confession of sins (and perhaps in the examination of conscience), asking the assembly to bow their heads for the blessing, and dismissing them. If the time of the individual confessions is lengthy, the deacon might assist the assembly in its prayer through a meditative reading of psalms and suitable Scripture passages.

The deacon may also preside at nonsacramental "penitential celebrations," when and where no priest is available to give sacramental absolution, or at any time. Such services, whose structure is that of a celebration of the Word of God, "are very helpful in promoting conversion of life and purification of heart" in preparation for sacramental absolution at a later time (no. 37). Certainly "care should be taken that the faithful do not confuse these celebrations with the celebration of the sacrament of penance" (no. 37). The content and purposes of penitential celebrations are described in the introduction to the Rite of Penance, nos. 36–37, and the rite includes models of such services for seasons and different categories of persons in Appendix II. Advent and Lent are excellent times for such services.

Marriage

Canon 1111 of the 1983 Code of Canon Law declares that "as long as they validly hold office, the local ordinary and the pastor can delegate to priests and deacons the faculty, even a general one, to assist at marriages within the limits of their territory" (par. 1).[40] While priests usually assist at weddings, a deacon may be asked to exercise his diaconal ministry in this sacramental celebration, especially if it takes place outside Mass or if he is related to the bride or groom. Directions for celebrating marriage outside Mass are found in nos. 39–54 of the Rite of Marriage.

Long before the service, the deacon might help the bride and groom plan the wedding liturgy by suggesting appropriate music, explaining alternate arrangements for the entrance procession (for example, one that includes the bride *and* groom, their parents, and bridesmaids and groomsmen walking as couples), and by discussing the options for Scripture readings, responsorial psalm, and other texts (presidential prayers, declaration of consent, blessing of rings, preface, nup-

---

40. *Code of Canon Law: Latin-English Edition*, translation prepared under the auspices of the Canon Law Society of America (Washington: Canon Law Society of America, 1983) 403.

tial blessing, concluding blessing). He might consult such planning guides as *Together for Life*, revised edition, particularly the special edition for marriage outside Mass (Notre Dame: Ave Maria Press, 2002), and *We Will Celebrate a Church Wedding* (Collegeville: Liturgical Press, 1983), and the video, *Preparing the Wedding Ceremony* (Collegeville: Liturgical Press, 1993), and make these resources available to the couple.

The Liturgy of the Word is not an insignificant prelude to the marriage rite. The readers should come to the wedding rehearsal twenty minutes early to practice their readings or practice them after the rehearsal. The deacon's homily on the readings should address the assembly generally and the couple particularly.

The rite of marriage, which follows the Liturgy of the Word, requires special care in its planning and great sensitivity in its celebration. According to the rubrics the assembly should stand throughout the ceremony, but they could be invited to sit so that they can see better. The wedding party might be arranged as follows:

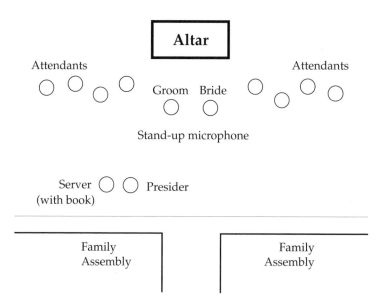

This arrangement highlights the bride and groom as the true ministers of the sacrament and makes their actions visible to all.

The deacon should suggest to the bride and groom that they face each other for their declaration of consent, join *both* their hands, and speak their vows to each other from memory (a card with the text in large letters, held by a server, can serve as a prompter if necessary). If the couple insists on repeating the vows after the deacon (or if their extreme nervousness requires this), adult-sized phrases should be used. The couple may also simply respond "I do" to the questions.

While the rite indicates that the general intercessions should be included, it provides no texts for them. Thus, the deacon should prepare intercessions tailored to the marriage celebration (GI, no. 70). In planning the liturgy with the bride and groom, he might suggest that they write the intercessions and provide some samples to assist them, or he could obtain from them a list of special intentions and persons they would like the assembly to pray for at their wedding, which could be included in the intercessions. The signing of the "marriage papers" should be deferred until after the service, since it is a purely legal matter extraneous to the liturgy.

Although the rite indicates that the nuptial blessing should immediately follow the Lord's Prayer, it might be moved to immediately after the exchange of rings or be used as the final prayer closing the general intercessions or as part of the final blessing at the end of the liturgy. It is fitting that the deacon lay his hands on the bride's head, on the groom's, and over both bride and groom, thus matching this gesture of blessing to the parts of the prayer. A server to hold the book is welcome here.

When presiding at the liturgy of marriage outside Mass, the deacon could invite the assembly to exchange a sign of peace after the Lord's Prayer and before the final blessing. If the congregation includes non-Roman Catholics, he might briefly explain the significance of this gesture before inviting them to exchange it. If the nuptial Mass cannot be celebrated but the assembly is Catholic, he could combine the marriage rite with a Communion service and preside according to the directions on pp. 71–77 of this booklet.

At the nuptial Mass the bride and groom, as well as other Roman Catholics who are present, may receive Communion under forms of both bread and wine. The deacon should be ready to minister the cup to the bride and groom, the members of the wedding party, and the assembly. The bride and groom should not serve as extraordinary ministers of Holy Communion (or readers or quasi-concelebrants at the altar), for their ministering the sacrament of marriage to each other is their unique service during this liturgy.

Even if there was a liturgical entrance procession at the beginning of the service, it is fitting that the presider and other ministers "fade out" at the end (there is no need for them to process out after the bride and groom).

Ordinations

The following remarks pertain to the diaconal role in ordinations other than the deacon's own. Before ministering in such celebrations or planning one's own, the deacon will want to consult the rite of ordination of deacons in the Roman Pontifical, the "Notes on the Celebration of the Rites of Ordination" in the Bishops' Committee on the Liturgy *Newsletter* XIX (November 1983) 42–44, and any diocesan guidelines.

The Eucharist with the rite of ordination to the diaconate or priesthood begins with the customary entrance procession, during which the deacon should carry the gospel book immediately in front of the candidates. The rite of ordination takes place after the Liturgy of the Word, in which the deacon exercises his ministry (especially proclaiming the gospel) as usual. Even if priests are present, he should exercise his proper ministry throughout the liturgy.

After the gospel reading the bishop takes his seat for the rite of ordination, which begins with the deacon calling the candidates for the order of deacon or priest: "Let those to be ordained deacons (or priests) come forward." Then he calls each candidate by his first and last name, to which each responds, "Present." The deacon may be expected to add "of the Order of St. _____ " or "of the Society of _____ " after names of professed religious. Then the candidates together go to the bishop, before whom they make a sign of reverence (usually a slight bow). The rite of ordination proceeds according to the rubrics in the Roman Pontifical.

The deacon should be prepared to signal changes of posture to the assembly, addressing them in the words "Let us kneel" immediately after the bishop's invitation to pray the Litany of Saints (except on Sundays and during the Easter season, when the assembly stands for the litany), and in the words "Let us stand" immediately after the bishop's prayer that concludes the litany. The deacon may also have to signal the assembly to stand or sit throughout the ordination rites, depending on how these have been planned.

Ordination of Deacons

Ordained deacons do not lay hands on the candidates after the bishop has done so, but their standing as an order at this service symbolizes a special relationship among themselves and with their bishop.

After the bishop's prayer of consecration, some of the assisting deacons or other ministers place a deacon's stole and a dalmatic on each of the newly ordained deacons ("Ordination of Deacons," no. 208). "Members of deacons' families do not vest the new deacons. The rite of vesting has been greatly simplified in the revised ordination rites and should not be unduly emphasized or prolonged."[41]

At the presentation of the gospel book to each new deacon, it is fitting that the bishop receive it from the ministering dea-

41. Bishops' Committee on the Liturgy *Newsletter*, XIX (November 1983) 44.

con's hands and place it in the hands of the new deacon, thus highlighting the collegiality of all deacons in heralding the Gospel of Christ. After the bishop gives the kiss of peace to each new deacon, the ministering deacon should do the same (if circumstances permit); the new deacons "do not greet their families during the kiss of peace which concludes the ordination rite, but may do so at the kiss of peace before communion."[42]

"In the Liturgy of the Eucharist the newly Ordained exercise their ministry for the first time as they assist the bishop, by preparing the altar, by giving Communion to the faithful, and particularly by offering the chalice, and proclaiming the instructions" ("Ordination of Deacons," no. 189). Of course, the "first string" of deacons who defer to the newly ordained ones remain vested and retain their seats in the sanctuary. The new deacons receive Communion under both kinds and assist the bishop in giving Communion to the assembly.

Ordination of Priests

After the bishop anoints the palms of the new priests, the deacon should be prepared to assist him in washing his hands at the chair (another minister may also assist).

He also assists the bishop in receiving the gifts of bread and wine as usual. Then, after preparing the bread on the paten (or plate, or in a ciborium) and the wine and water in the chalice, he brings the paten and chalice to the bishop, who presents them to each new priest as he kneels before him.

The ministry of new priest-concelebrants should not interfere with the deacon's ministry. What the General Instruction says about diaconal ministry at a concelebrated Mass applies to the liturgy of ordination: the concelebrants "should not be in the deacon's way whenever he needs to go to the altar to perform his ministry" (no. 215) and should not appropriate his functions even on their ordination day.

42. Ibid.

Pastoral Care and Visitation of the Sick

At present Roman Catholic deacons have not been authorized to minister the sacrament of anointing. Nevertheless, like their predecessors in second-century Rome, they are authorized to bring Communion to the sick and viaticum to the dying. The revised rites for the visitation and Communion of the sick are contained in Pastoral Care of the Sick: Rites of Anointing and Viaticum (1983), especially nos. 71–96, 161–88, and 197–222. Some helpful suggestions for the ministry of Communion to the sick and confined are found in the Liturgical Press booklet *The Ministry of Communion*, pp. 21–25, but note the special characteristics of giving Communion as viaticum in nos. 175–83, 186–88, and 197–211 of the rite.

The deacon's service to the priest and to the sick during a communal celebration of anointing sets a seal upon his regular ministry to the sick in their homes, nursing homes, and hospitals. He might read the Scripture lessons (certainly the gospel) and preach. He should hold the book for the priest during the prayers and especially during the blessing of the oil; thus the priest can take the oil in his hands and hold it high enough for all to see it during the prayer of blessing. He should accompany the priest as he anoints each person, carrying the oil and a small card with the prayer of anointing on it in large letters. This will free the priest to maximize his gestures during the anointing. After the anointing, the deacon assists the priest in washing his hands with water and quartered lemons. If the communal anointing takes place at Mass, the deacon should be especially attentive to the needs of disabled and infirm persons during Communion. If the priest is to conclude the service with a solemn blessing or prayer over the people, the deacon should ask the assembly to bow their heads as usual and dismiss them after the blessing, commending the sick to their care (see no. 148 of the rite).

Funerals

"When no priest is available, deacons, as ministers of the Word, of the altar, and of charity, preside at funeral rites" (Order of Christian Funerals, no. 14). Thus, familiarity with the rubrics and texts for the liturgy of Christian burial, especially Part I of the Order of Christian Funerals, is necessary for presiding at the wake service and the cemetery service. A deacon might also preside at the service in church (perhaps with Communion) when the funeral Mass cannot be celebrated. Some helpful resources are H. Richard Rutherford, *The Order of Christian Funerals: An Invitation to Pastoral Care* (Collegeville: Liturgical Press, 1990) and the set of three videos, *Understanding the Order of Christian Funerals* (Collegeville: Liturgical Press, 1997).

The wake service (or vigil service) takes the form of a celebration of the Word of God and is usually held in a mortuary or chapel. Directions and texts are found in nos. 51–81 of the rite. Many morticians provide prayer cards or booklets (sometimes several different ones) for these services. "Whenever possible, the family of the deceased should take part in the selection of texts and music and in the designation of liturgical ministers" for the vigil (Order of Christian Funerals, no. 65). If such consultation is difficult or impossible, the deacon is free to use the suggested texts and available materials, or to prepare a service of psalms, readings, intercessions, and song that corresponds to the outline given in the rite and that facilitates the participation of the worshipers. A brief homily seems very appropriate and appreciated. Solemn blessing no. 20 from the Roman Missal ("The Dead") would be a fitting conclusion to the vigil service. While such a celebration of the Word is the normative form of vigil service, the family of the deceased person may express a strong preference for the traditional recitation of the Rosary. The deacon should know the form and content of this prayer. Both the celebration of the Word and the Rosary could be part of the vigil service if the deacon suggests to the family that he could lead the former and others (for example, members of parish societies) could lead the latter.

At the funeral Mass the deacon's assistance to the priest reflects the role of minister of consolation that he shares with him. The deacon accompanies the priest and other ministers to the door of the church and takes his place at the head of the deceased person. He invites the worshipers in the church to turn and welcome the body. When the casket reaches its place before the altar, the deacon joins the priest in bowing to the altar and kissing it before moving to the chair for the opening prayer. During the Liturgy of the Word, he exercises his usual ministry: proclaiming the gospel, possibly preaching, and leading the general intercessions (unless a relative or friend of the deceased person is to do this).

If incense is used during the preparation of the gifts and the altar, the deacon assists the priest as usual. The priest should complete the incensing of the altar before proceeding to incense the body. The deacon should accompany him during the incensing, and then either he or another minister should incense the priest and the assembly. If they are slow to stand for the incensing, a gracious upward gesture with the hand can be a polite invitation to do so.

The deacon's ministry during the Liturgy of the Eucharist is the same as that during any Mass. If there are any announcements regarding the procession to the cemetery or luncheon after the burial, they should be made immediately after the prayer after Communion. When the final commendation and farewell is celebrated in the church after Mass, the deacon stands with the priest and other ministers near the casket, and accompanies the priest in the procession to the cemetery.

When all have gathered in the cemetery, the priest says a prayer for blessing the grave or tomb (if it has not been blessed). The deacon assists him if he is to sprinkle the casket and grave or tomb with holy water and incense them (the sprinkling and incensing, ideally done by circling the casket, may be part of the final commendation if it is celebrated at the grave or tomb). If the intercessions are to follow, he should lead them; the priest will conclude them with the Lord's Prayer, followed by another prayer. There follows a "prayer over the people," before which the deacon says: "Bow your heads and pray for God's blessing." The priest then speaks the familiar "Eternal rest grant unto him (her), O Lord," (in which it is fitting to replace "him" or "her" with the first name of the deceased person), and the assembly's response. The rite of committal at the cemetery concludes with a blessing (form A is used by a priest or deacon), but an appropriate song (for example, "To Jesus Christ, Our Sovereign King") is welcome. The folding and presentation of the flag and other military ceremonies should be deferred until after the liturgical rites. If there is a custom of inviting relatives and friends to sprinkle the casket with holy water, the deacon assists them by giving them the sprinkler.

When a funeral Mass cannot be celebrated, the deacon may preside at the funeral service consisting of a Liturgy of the Word (possibly with Communion) and the final commendation, and also at the cemetery service. The opening rites are identical to those at the funeral mass, but note the expanded invitation to prayer in no. 189. As many as three Scripture readings may be used, the first of them taken from the Old Testament (except during the Easter season, when a text from the Acts of the Apostles or the book of Revelation is used). After the homily, the general intercessions are concluded with a prayer by the presider, followed by the Lord's Prayer by all. The final commendation and farewell may be celebrated immediately after this service or be deferred until the cemetery service, which takes place as described above.

Holy Communion outside Mass

More and more we have seen the Communion service, presided over by a deacon or layperson, substituted for the Mass in parishes without priests. Is the Communion service a poor substitute for the Mass? No, in the sense that both of these official liturgies of the Church celebrate Christ's saving death and resurrection and enable us to share in them by receiving his Body and Blood. But the worldwide phenomenon of parishes without priests to serve them and preside at the Sunday Eucharist raises some serious questions about the Communion service as a regular form of parish worship.

In the traditional observance of Sunday in the Church, there ideally come together three key elements: time, community, and event. In other words, on the Lord's *day*, the Lord's *people* celebrate the Lord's *supper*. Where this ideal form of Sunday worship becomes impossible, the ministry of deacons and lay leaders is becoming customary. This practice has been a controversial one, however. Many have raised questions such as: If the Communion service becomes the usual Sunday or weekday worship in priestless parishes, will not the people's experience of giving thanks over bread and cup be diminished or lost? Will not the Eucharist increasingly be seen as a thing given to them, not an action done by them?

The complete eucharistic celebration on Sunday is a full expression of the priestly calling of the entire people of God and is a centuries-old Roman Catholic tradition. To what extent are we prepared to depart from it in favor of Communion services on Sunday? This is a debate that will continue for some time in the Church. In the meantime, many deacons and extraordinary ministers of Holy Communion will be called upon to lead such services in their parish communities.

Practical Suggestions

The basic rite according to which you lead Communion services is contained in the 1973 document *Holy Communion and Worship of the Eucharist outside Mass* (henceforth referred to as *Holy Communion*). But you will also want to be familiar with the *Directory for Sunday Celebrations in the Absence of a Priest* (henceforth referred to as *Directory*) if you preside at such celebrations, and with the rite for the United States based on the *Directory's* provisions.

The presentation of the gifts and the Eucharistic Prayer are not included in a Communion service, but nothing prescribed or beneficial should be lacking in this rite (for example, a full liturgy of the Word and music, if possible) or in your leadership (for example, revealing God's graciousness to the worshipers through your words and gestures). Good presiders are like clear glass vessels that do not obscure, but rather reveal the contents of the liturgy. A fine crystal goblet enhances the appearance of the wine inside it, but the cartoon characters on a glass call attention to themselves. Presiding at a Communion service means doing everything one can to help a holy people to receive the holy gift of Eucharist. The roles of reader, cantor, etc., are to be shared among suitable persons (*Directory*, no. 40).

Your vesture should be an alb and a stole in the color proper to the season or feast.

Introductory Rites

The *Directory* does not indicate the content of these rites, while *Holy Communion* (nos. 27–28) generally follows the Order of Mass.

An opening hymn or gathering music, as well as an entrance procession, are not prescribed in either document, but singing at the beginning of the service can help unify the assembly. The sign of the cross, also not prescribed, would seem to be fitting at this time. See *Holy Communion*, no. 27, for a suggested form of greeting, but you may prepare your own. You might think of "greeting" as being equivalent to brief introductory words that help the assembled worshipers focus their hearts and minds on this *particular* celebration: sharing the Body and Blood of Christ on this feast or occasion.

Next follows the penitential rite (*Holy Communion*, no. 28), for which the Roman Missal includes three forms.

An opening prayer is not prescribed for ordinary celebrations, but the *Directory* states that on Sundays and solemnities the opening prayer and the prayer after Communion are taken from the Roman Missal (no. 36).

Celebration of the Word of God

One or more readings from Scripture follow the introductory rites. They are taken "either from the Mass of the day or from the votive Masses of the Holy Eucharist or the Precious Blood," which are found in the Lectionary for Mass (*Holy Communion*, no. 29). See *Holy Communion*, nos. 113–88, for an extensive list of possible and appropriate readings (for example, those for the votive Mass of the Sacred Heart). On Sundays and solemnities the readings assigned to the day in the Lectionary are used (*Directory*, no. 36).

After the first reading there is a psalm, song, or silent prayer. The acclamation before the gospel is not prescribed, but is very appropriate. If it is used, it should be sung.

Preaching is optional, but certainly welcome in order to better nourish the assembly from the two tables of Word and sacrament. The profession of faith is normally recited on Sundays and solemnities. The general intercessions conclude the celebration of the Word.

Thanksgiving

The *Directory* prescribes a "Thanksgiving" as part of the rite on Sundays, but this element would be fitting on other days as well. The thanksgiving takes one of the following forms: (a) After the general intercessions or after the sharing of Communion, the presider invites the assembly to an act of thanksgiving, which may be: a psalm (for example, Pss 100, 113, 118, 136, 147, or 150), a hymn or canticle (for example the *Glory to God*, or Mary's *Magnificat*), or a litany sung or recited by all present. The presider and the assembly stand facing the altar for the thanksgiving; (b)

Alternatively, before the Lord's Prayer that begins the Communion rite, the presider takes the Eucharist from the place of reservation, places it on the altar, and genuflects. Then, while kneeling before the sacrament, all sing or recite a hymn, psalm, or litany directed to Christ in the Eucharist. Your parish music ministers might be asked to suggest and lead suitable music.

The thanksgiving is not to take the form of a Eucharistic Prayer, nor are the prefaces and Eucharistic Prayers of the Roman Missal to be used (*Directory*, no. 45). This is to avoid confusing the Communion service with the full eucharistic celebration.

Communion Rite

The reserved Eucharist is taken from the tabernacle, placed on the altar, and honored with a genuflection.

The Lord's Prayer, introduced by the presider and sung or recited by all, now follows, unless the act of thanksgiving is to take place first (see *Directory*, no. 45). The words, "Deliver us, Lord, from every evil. . . ." are omitted. After the Lord's Prayer, the sign of peace is optional but welcome preparation for sharing Communion. Extend your hands widely, embracing the assembly, as you give the invitation, "Let us offer each other the sign of peace." Then share with those around you the ritual gesture that seals our unity in the peace of Christ.

After genuflecting, raise a piece of the consecrated bread over the plate and say, "This is the Lamb of God. . . ." (*Holy Communion*, no. 32). Wait for the assembly to respond, "Lord, I am not worthy. . . ." before receiving Communion.

The directions indicate that the presider and other ministers are to receive Communion before serving the assembly. During the sharing of Communion, a hymn may be sung.

When Communion is finished, the unused bread is gathered into containers at the altar or side table for placement in the tabernacle, the transfer to which might be done by an extraordinary minister of Holy Communion. Crumbs should be disposed of reverently, either by consuming them or by mixing them with water and drinking the mixture, or by pouring it into the sacrarium. It is preferable that all Communion vessels be cleansed in the sacristy after the liturgy.

After the sharing of Communion, there may be a period of silence, or a psalm or song of praise may be sung (*Holy Communion*, no. 37). The *Directory* suggests various forms of thanksgiving at this point (no. 45). Any necessary announcements should be made before the concluding prayer, for which a number of options are provided (*Holy Communion*, nos. 38, 210–22). On Sundays and solemnities this prayer should be the one assigned to the day in the Roman Missal.

Concluding Rites

In concluding the Communion service, a deacon invokes God's blessing on the assembly with one of the texts given in *Holy Communion* (no. 40).

According to the *Directory* (no. 39), a lay presider is to omit the dismissal. But *Holy Communion* (no. 41) provides a dismissal ("Go in the peace of Christ") for use by the minister, presumably either ordained or lay.

An exit procession would be fitting only if there has been an entrance procession. As the procession forms, make the customary reverence to the altar (a low bow, or a genuflection if the tabernacle is behind the altar), and leave the sanctuary in the same order as at the beginning of the service. A final hymn or recessional music is not prescribed, but might help send the assembly forth to love and serve the Lord in the members of his body.

The following outline lists the elements of the rite of giving Holy Communion outside Mass with the celebration of the Word. Parts in [ ] are fitting but not required according to the official rite.

Introductory Rites

- — [Opening hymn or gathering music]
- — Greeting
- — Penitential Rite
- — [Opening Prayer]

Celebration of the Word of God

- — One or more readings from Scripture
- — Psalm following first reading, or song or silent prayer
- — [Gospel Acclamation before Gospel]
- — [Homily]
- — General Intercessions

Holy Communion

- — Reserved Eucharist is brought to the altar, followed by genuflection
- — Lord's Prayer
- — Sign of peace may be exchanged
- — Genuflection before "This is the Lamb of God. . . ."
- — Giving of Communion, during which a hymn may be sung
- — Eucharist is returned to the tabernacle
- — Silence, or a psalm or song of praise may be sung
- — Concluding Prayer, for which all stand (14 options)

Concluding Rite

- — Blessing (simple, solemn, or prayer over the people)
- — Dismissal
- — [Final hymn or recessional music]

Exposition and Benediction of the Blessed Sacrament

The service called "Benediction" takes its name from the blessing with the Blessed Sacrament that concludes it. The "Rite of Eucharistic Exposition and Benediction" is contained in Holy Communion and Worship of the Eucharist Outside Mass, nos. 79–100.

In a sense, Benediction is the Mass in stop-action: it enables worshipers to dwell upon Christ's self-gift in the Eucharist a bit longer, directing them backward to the Mass from which the Blessed Sacrament comes and forward to the next Mass in which they receive this sacrament. Thus, exposition is not to occur during or at the same time as Mass in the same area of the church (no. 83), nor is it to occur for the purpose of the blessing alone, that is, without "prayers, songs and readings to direct the attention of the faithful to the worship of Christ the Lord" (nos. 89, 95). Parts of the Liturgy of the Hours may be celebrated if the exposition is lengthy (no. 96).

"The ordinary minister for exposition of the eucharist is a priest or deacon. At the end of the period of adoration, before the reposition, he blesses the people with the sacrament" (no. 91). Instituted acolytes and extraordinary ministers of Holy Communion may expose the sacrament, but may not give the blessing with it.

The directions for vesture indicate that a priest or deacon "should vest in an alb or surplice over a cassock, and a stole" and "should wear a white cope and humeral veil to give the blessing at the end of adoration, when the exposition takes place with the monstrance; in the case of exposition in the ciborium, the humeral veil should be worn" (no. 92). Before the service, wearing the cope and putting on the humeral veil should be practiced.

When the exposition is done with the monstrance, four to six candles are used and incense is required; when it is done with the ciborium, at least two candles are used and incense is optional (no. 85). A single genuflection (one knee) is made before the Blessed Sacrament, whether it is reserved in the tabernacle or exposed for public adoration (no. 84).

Before the service, the large host for the monstrance should be placed in a metal and glass clip called a *luna* or *lunella*. In some places this host customarily has been reserved in a small container (*custodia*) on the altar prior to the service, but often the host is reserved in the tabernacle as usual.

Directions for servers are included in the Liturgical Press booklet *The Ministry of Servers*, 25–28. As the service begins, the presider processes from the sacristy or back of the church to the altar, following the servers. "If the holy eucharist is not reserved at the altar where the exposition is to take place, the minister puts on a humeral veil and brings the sacrament from the place of reservation; he is accompanied by servers or by the faithful with lighted candles" (no. 93). He genuflects before the tabernacle, removes the large host, and closes the tabernacle; then he returns to the altar, places the host in the monstrance, and turns the monstrance toward the assembly.

After the presider has returned to the sanctuary floor, the servers should remove the humeral veil. He places incense in the censer, kneels before the Blessed Sacrament, bows, incenses the Blessed Sacrament with three triple swings of the censer, bows again, and returns the censer to the server. He genuflects and takes his seat in the sanctuary for the prayers, songs, and readings. He reads the gospel lesson if one has been selected for the service; if he chooses to preach a homily, he may do so from the lectern or from his chair.

At the conclusion of the service, the presider returns to the middle of the altar and genuflects. He places incense in the censer, kneels, bows, incenses the Blessed Sacrament, bows again, and returns the censer to the server. He stands and sings or says the appointed prayer, for which the rite provides seven options in nos. 98, 224–29. He kneels, receives the humeral veil from the server, stands, genuflects, and ascends the altar steps. Taking the monstrance in his hands and wrapping the veil around its base, he reverently makes a large sign of the cross (in silence) over the assembly and replaces the monstrance on the altar. The "Divine Praises" ("Blessed be God") are a customary (but not obligatory) litany of praise following the blessing; if he chooses to lead these acclamatory prayers, he returns to the altar step and kneels for them (the server should remove the humeral veil before the prayers begin).

The service concludes with reposition (returning the Blessed Sacrament to the tabernacle). The presider ascends the altar steps and removes the Blessed Sacrament from the monstrance. He may place it in the small container on the altar or return it to the tabernacle (in the latter case, he receives the humeral veil from the server before the reposition begins). He follows the servers in procession to the tabernacle, places the Blessed Sacrament inside, closes the tabernacle, genuflects, and returns to the sacristy.

Liturgy of the Hours

At the ordination of a deacon, the bishop asks: "Do (all of) you resolve to maintain and deepen the spirit of prayer that is proper to your way of life and, in keeping with this spirit and what is required of you, to celebrate faithfully the Liturgy of the Hours with and for the People of God and indeed for the whole world?" ("Ordination of Deacons," no. 200). The deacon's "I do," which expresses his commitment to the Church's official prayer, takes visible form when he assists or presides at public services of morning and evening prayer.

Some of the elements of evening prayer that the nun Egeria described in the fourth century are contained in the following suggested, unofficial form of evening prayer for parishes based on the official Liturgy of the Hours.

"The priest or deacon who presides at a celebration may wear a stole over the alb or surplice; a priest may also wear a cope" (General Instruction of the Liturgy of the Hours, no. 255); there seems to be no reason why a presiding deacon could not wear a cope (as at baptism).

During the entrance procession, the deacon carries the Easter candle (or other large candle in Lent) through the darkened church, preceded by a minister swinging a smoking censer, and followed by a reader carrying the Lectionary or Bible; the cantor; and the presider.

After the others have venerated the altar, the deacon begins the light service by facing the assembly, holding the candle high, and singing or saying the light proclamation, for example, "Light and peace in Jesus Christ our Lord." After all have responded, "Thanks be to God!" he places the candle in its stand. Then, as all sing an evening hymn with the theme of light and the lights in the church are turned up, he lights the altar candles and other candles in the church (for example, those on the Advent wreath, or those before Mary's image on a Marian feast).

Psalm 141, the classic "theme psalm" for evening prayer, follows, during which all stand and sing a refrain while the cantor sings the verses. As this psalm is being sung, the deacon places incense in the censer; then he moves through the assembly, incensing it in a gesture of repentance and purification, or simply allows the fragrant smoke to ascend from the stationary censer. After the psalm the presider sings or says, "Let us pray." All make the words and sentiments of the psalm the basis of their silent prayer; then the presider sings or says a "psalm-prayer" or "collect" that gathers up the silent prayers of all into one that he offers in their name.

There follow other sung psalms with refrains (especially those geared to the time of day, season, or feast), for which all are seated. The pattern "Let us pray"—silent prayer—psalm-prayer is repeated after each psalm. It is customary to stand for the psalm-prayers, but if many of the worshipers are elderly, only the presider and deacon might stand for these prayers. The final psalm (perhaps in hymnic form), or a canticle from the Pauline letters or the Book of Revelation, should conclude with a Trinitarian doxology, and thus the psalm-prayer is omitted. All should stand for this final psalm or canticle.

Then the reader proclaims a brief reading from Scripture (only a few verses). All sit for this reading, which may be chosen from the Old or New Testament, in accord with the season or feast. Gospel readings should not be chosen because they are reserved for the Eucharist (General Instruction of the Liturgy of the Hours, no. 158).

A brief homily (a minute or two) on the reading is optional, but would be most fitting on Sundays and greater feasts. A period of silent reflection should follow.

The Canticle of the Blessed Virgin Mary, the *Magnificat* (Luke 1:46-55) has traditionally served as the highpoint of evening prayer. The Canticle of Simeon, the *Nunc dimittis* (Luke 2:29-32), the traditional canticle for night prayer, might be substituted if the service takes place later in the evening. All stand for the gospel canticle and make the sign of the cross at the beginning (the deacon should gesture for the assembly to stand if they are slow to do so). He brings the censer to the presider, assists in placing incense, and accompanies the presider as he incenses the candle, altar, cross, and assembly.

Leading the intercessions is the deacon's proper role, but he might defer to a cantor on occasion. He could conclude the prepared intentions by inviting the assembly to include their spontaneous ones. He gathers these together in words like, "For all these intentions, let us pray to the Lord," so that all can respond with a final "Lord, hear our prayer" or "Lord, have mercy." The Lord's Prayer, introduced by the presider and sung or said by all, concludes the intercessions.

The presider says a final prayer (for example, the opening prayer from the Mass of the day or a seasonal prayer), and the deacon makes any necessary announcements (for example, the times and places of future liturgical services).

An appropriate solemn blessing (taken from the Roman Missal or newly composed) is very fitting, for which the deacon should invite the assembly to bow their heads. At its conclusion, he could invite the assembly to exchange a sign of peace. While the official Liturgy of the Hours ends with a dismissal by the deacon, "Go in peace," this does not seem necessary.

As the sign of peace is ending, a final hymn or postlude may begin, during which the ministers bow to the altar and exit (the presider and deacon walk together at the end of the procession).

The service outlined here would be especially fitting on the Sundays of the Advent, Christmas, Lent, and Easter seasons, as well as on the greater feasts (for example, the parish's patronal feast). It could also be a prayerful conclusion to the celebrations on a deacon's ordination day.

If assisting the presider, the deacon carries the candle with dignity during the entrance procession and light service, assists with the book and censer, gives necessary directions to the assembly (and to the other ministers if necessary), leads the intercessions, and makes announcements. If he is presiding, he also prays the psalm-prayers in a loud and clear voice, preaches a brief but well-crafted homily on the Scripture reading, introduces the Lord's Prayer, says the final prayer, and gives the blessing.

Way of the Cross

The popular devotion known as the Way of the Cross, or Stations, celebrates what we profess in the Nicene Creed: for our sake Jesus Christ "was crucified under Pontius Pilate; he suffered, died, and was buried." But having been raised to life as our Savior, Christ gives us a share in that life. That is why we meditate on his sufferings and death, the necessary prelude to his resurrection (and ours): "If we have died with him we shall also live with him" (2 Tim 2:11).

The Way of the Cross is a processional service in which the priest or deacon and the servers (usually three) move through the church and stop in front of fourteen crosses or images that recall some events in the last hours of Jesus' life. At each station there may be a brief reading from Scripture or a meditation on Jesus' Passion, and a prayer or two; a verse of a song (traditionally, "At the Cross Her Station Keeping") accompanies the movement from station to station. These texts are usually provided in a booklet for use during the service. The distinctive way in which each parish celebrates this devotion seems to be handed on from generation to generation, and the deacon will want to acquaint himself with it before he presides.

Customary vesture is an alb and stole, and also a cope if desired (especially if Benediction of the Blessed Sacrament is to follow). The traditional vestment color is purple (the color of penitence) but red (the color of the Passion, thus used on Good Friday) seems more fitting.

Directions for servers are included in the Liturgical Press booklet *The Ministry of Servers*, 22–24. In processing from the sacristy, the presider follows the crossbearer and candlebearers to the front of the altar. After bowing or genuflecting, he kneels or stands to say the opening prayer in the booklet (there may also be a prayer for the assembly to recite). He follows the servers to the first station, turns toward the image, and announces the number and title of the station as given in the booklet, for example, "The first station: Jesus is condemned to death." Then he could invite the assembly to pray for a particular group of suffering people, for example, at the first station: "Let us pray for those condemned to death for their witness to truth and justice." In this way the assembly might offer their priestly intercession for those who suffer with Christ as well as their own repentance for the suffering they have caused others. The presider might help the liturgy committee prepare such a list of intentions for the fourteen stations and then include the intentions on the proper pages of his booklet.

After announcing the number and title of the station (and perhaps an intention), the presider makes a prolonged genuflection as he says, "We adore you, O Christ, and we praise you," and as the people respond, "Because by your holy cross you have redeemed the world." He alone should read the short Scripture passage or meditation aloud; the entire assembly prays the following prayer aloud, so the pace should be gauged accordingly.

During the verse of the song, the presider follows the servers to the next station. He could invite the assembly to kneel for the reading and prayer at the twelfth station (Jesus dies on the cross) just as they do on Palm Sunday of the Lord's Passion and Good Friday after the death of Jesus is recounted in the reading of the Passion.

After the procession has stopped in front of all the stations and returned to the sanctuary, the presider kneels or stands in front of the altar and leads the assembly in the closing prayer. If there is a fifteenth station (the resurrection of Jesus) in the booklet but not on the station route of the church, the presider could make it before the tabernacle, the "station" of the fullness of Christ's paschal mystery in which we share (he could also lead the closing prayer there). To conclude the service, he bows or genuflects and follows the servers to the sacristy.

Holy Week Liturgies
(in addition to usual diaconal functions)

The following general outlines, based on the Roman Missal's rubrics, summarize the deacon's role in the liturgies of Holy Week. In addition to these outlines, each deacon will want to know the particular worship space, liturgical adaptations, and local customs of these celebrations in his own parish or community.

Palm Sunday of the Lord's Passion

Procession

— Wear a red stole (and dalmatic if available).

— Assist the priest as he blesses and sprinkles the palms.

— Proclaim the gospel of the entry into Jerusalem (the proper one for cycle A, B, or C).

— Give necessary directions for the procession and make the announcement to begin it.

— Accompany the priest at the beginning or end of the procession.

Mass

— Read the Passion (the proper one for cycle A, B, or C), omitting the usual greeting, signs of the cross, and conclusion (lay readers may assist in this reading).

Easter Triduum

Holy Thursday

Evening Mass of the Lord's Supper

— Wear a white stole (and dalmatic if available).

— During the washing of feet, invite the participants to come forward and show them to their places in the sanctuary; assist the priest by carrying the bowl or pitcher from person to person.

— Make sure that the ciborium with consecrated bread for Good Friday remains on the altar after Communion.

Transfer of the Holy Eucharist

— Assist the priest in placing incense; kneel as he incenses the Blessed Sacrament; place the humeral veil on his shoulders.

— Accompany the priest to the place of reposition; assist him in placing incense; kneel during incensing; after the tabernacle is closed, genuflect with the priest and return to the sacristy.

Adoration

— Assist or preside at prayer services during the period of adoration, especially a night prayer service to close this time; after this service, remove the Blessed Sacrament to the sacristy where it will be kept for Communion on Good Friday.

Good Friday

— Besides assisting or presiding at the Celebration of the Lord's Passion, assist or preside at a public celebration of morning prayer or noon prayer, as well as the Way of the Cross.

Celebration of the Lord's Passion

— Wear a red stole (and dalmatic if available).

Entrance

— Reverence the altar with the priest, and prostrate or kneel for silent prayer.
— Stand for the opening prayer, and invite the assembly to stand if they are slow to do so.

Liturgy of the Word

— Read the Passion according to John (invariable), omitting the usual greeting, signs of the cross, and conclusion (lay readers may assist in this reading).
— Give the invitation to kneel and stand during the solemn intercessions and perhaps announce the intentions.

Veneration of the Cross

— Form I: Slowly process to the altar carrying the veiled cross, and there uncover it in three stages, lifting it high and singing on a higher pitch each time: "This is the wood of the cross, on which hung the Savior of the world"; or sing the words recto-tono with an inflection at the end. Then carry the cross to the place where veneration will occur.

— Form II: Slowly process to the altar carrying the unveiled cross. Stop near the entrance to the church, in the middle of the church, and at the entrance to the sanctuary, lift the cross high each time and sing on a higher pitch each time: "This is the wood of the cross . . . ." Then carry the cross to the place where veneration will occur.

— Give necessary directions for individual veneration of the cross and venerate the cross after the priest.

Holy Communion

— After the altar is covered with a cloth and corporal and the Roman Missal is placed on it, bring the ciborium with the Blessed Sacrament from the place of reposition (or sacristy); place the ciborium on the altar and uncover it; signal the priest to approach the altar for the Communion rite; after Communion remove the Blessed Sacrament to the sacristy or to the tabernacle.

— Invite the assembly to bow their heads for the prayer over the people, but do not give a dismissal.

— Genuflect to the cross during the exit procession.

Holy Saturday

— In addition to assisting at the Easter Vigil, assist or preside at a public celebration of morning prayer or noon prayer.

Easter Vigil

— Wear a white stole (and dalmatic if available).

Service of Light

— Carry the Easter candle to the place where the fire will be blessed.

— Hold the lit candle high and lead the procession into the church, stopping three times: where the fire is blessed, at the church door (or midway through the church, if the fire is blessed at the church door), and in the sanctuary (facing the people). Lift the candle high and sing "Christ our Light" on a higher pitch each time; after the second response, lower the candle so that the ministers and assembly can light their candles from it.

— Place the candle in its stand and assist the priest in placing incense. If singing the Easter Proclamation (*Exsultet*), ask the priest for the blessing, and then incense the candle (walking around it if possible) and the book containing the text; after concluding the Easter Proclamation, return to the priest's side for the Liturgy of the Word.

Liturgy of the Word

— Invite the assembly to stand for the prayers after the psalms between the readings if they are slow to do so.

— Proclaim the gospel for the Vigil (the proper one for cycle A, B, or C).

Liturgy of Baptism

— During the ceremonies, render helpful assistance to candidates, parents, and godparents, as well as to the priest.

— Perhaps assist the priest in sprinkling the assembly with the blessed water.

— Include the names of the newly baptized and of those received into full communion in the general intercessions.

Liturgy of the Eucharist

— Sing or say the dismissal with the double "Alleluia."

Petitions for Deacons from Ancient Liturgies

"Make the deacons holy too. Let them be pure in heart and body, that they may be able to fulfill their ministry with a pure conscience and present the sacred body and blood (of the Lord)."

*— from a litany in the eucharistic liturgy
of Bishop Serapion (d. 362?)*[43]

"Let us pray for all deacons and ministers of Christ. May God grant them to serve him without fault."

*— from a litany in the eucharistic liturgy
in Apostolic Constitutions, VIII, 10, 1-22*[44]

43. Q. in Deiss, 191.
44. Q. in ibid., 225.

Prayer before Ministering at the Eucharist

The following prayer, based on an opening prayer from the Roman Missal's Mass "For the Priest Himself," is fitting for a deacon to use before ministering at the Eucharist:

> God of mercy,
> hear my prayers,
> and fill my heart with the light
>   of your Holy Spirit.
> May I worthily minister your mysteries,
> faithfully serve your Church,
> and come to love you with a never-ending love.
>
> Grant this through our Lord Jesus Christ, your Son,
> who lives and reigns with you and the Holy Spirit,
> one God, for ever and ever. Amen.

Prayer after Ministering at the Eucharist

The following prayer, based on a prayer after Communion from the Roman Missal's Mass "For the Priest Himself," is fitting for a deacon to use after ministering at the Eucharist:

> Father,
> you strengthen me with bread from heaven
> and give me the joy of sharing the cup of the new
>   covenant.
> Keep me faithful in your service
> and let me spend my entire life working with courage
>   and love
> for the salvation of humanity.
>
> Grant this through Christ our Lord. Amen.

Suggestions for Further Reading

History and Theology of Diaconal Ministry

Barnett, James M. *The Diaconate: A Full and Equal Order*. New York: The Seabury Press, 1979.

Bishops' Committee on the Liturgy. *Study Text VI: The Deacon, Minister of Word and Sacrament*. Washington: United States Catholic Conference, 1979.

Echlin, Edward P. *The Deacon in the Church: Past and Future*. Staten Island: Alba House, 1971.

———. "The Deacon's Golden Age." *Worship* 45 (January 1971) 37–46.

———. "The Origins of the Permanent Diaconate." *The American Ecclesiastical Record* (August 1970) 92–106.

Liturgical Ministry: Diaconate. Vol. 13 (Winter 2004).

Porter, H. Boone. "A Traditional Reflection on Diaconate in Relation to 'Omnivorous Priesthood.'" *Living Worship* 12 (November 1976).

Rahner, Karl. "The Theology of the Restoration of the Diaconate." *Theological Investigations*, vol. V. Trans. Karl H. Kruger. Baltimore: Helicon Press, 1966, 268–314.

Vallee, Sherri L. "The Diaconate Question." *Ministry and Liturgy* 31 (August 2004) 11–13.

Presiding and Assisting

Brooks-Leonard, John. *Leading the Community in Prayer: The Art of Presiding for Deacons and Lay Persons*. VHS videocassette. Collegeville: Liturgical Press, 1990.

Hovda, Robert W. *Strong, Loving and Wise: Presiding in Liturgy*. Collegeville: Liturgical Press, 1980.

Hughes, Kathleen. *Lay Presiding: The Art of Leading Prayer*. Collegeville: Liturgical Press, 1991.

Kavanagh, Aidan. *Elements of Rite: A Handbook of Liturgical Style*. New York: Pueblo Publishing Company, 1982; Collegeville: Liturgical Press, 1990.

Kwatera, Michael. *The Ministry of Communion*. 2nd ed. Collegeville: Liturgical Press, 2004.

———. *The Ministry of Servers*. 2nd ed. Collegeville: Liturgical Press, 2004.

Proclaiming the Scriptures

Keifer, Ralph. *To Hear and Proclaim: Introduction to the Roman Lectionary*. With Commentary for Musicians and Priests. Washington: NPM Publications, 1983.

Lonergan, Ray. *A Well-Trained Tongue*. Chicago: Liturgy Training Publications, 1983.

Meyer, Marty. *Skills for Lectors*. Chicago: Liturgy Training Publications, 1981.

Walker, William O., Jr., gen. ed. *The HarperCollins Bible Pronunciation Guide*. HarperSan Francisco, 1994.

Wallace, James A. *The Ministry of Lectors*. 2nd ed. Collegeville: Liturgical Press, 2004.

Workbook for Lectors and Gospel Readers. Chicago: Archdiocese of Chicago, Liturgy Training Publications. Yearly editions.

Preaching

Bishops' Committee on Priestly Life and Ministry. *Fulfilled in Your Hearing: The Homily in the Sunday Assembly*. Washington: United States Catholic Conference, 1982.

Cormier, Jay. *Giving Good Homilies: A Communications Guide for More Effective Preaching*. Notre Dame: Ave Maria Press, 1984.

Edwards, O. C., Jr. *Elements of Homiletic: A Method for Preparing to Preach*. New York: Pueblo Publishing Company, 1982; Collegeville: Liturgical Press, 1990.

Skudlarek, William. *The Word in Worship: Preaching in a Liturgical Context*. Abingdon Preacher's Library. Nashville: Abingdon, 1981.

Sloyan, Gerard S. *Worshipful Preaching*. Philadelphia: Fortress Press, 1984.